THE DIGEST BOOK OF
Upland Game Hunting

By
Bob Bell

DBI Books Inc., Northfield, Illinois

For Peej,
who deserves far more

ISBN 0-695-81319-6   Library of Congress Catalog Card Number 79-84931

Table of Contents

CHAPTER 1
Ruffed Grouse 5

CHAPTER 2
Woodcock 15

CHAPTER 3
Cottontail Rabbits 21

CHAPTER 4
Snowshoe Rabbits 32

CHAPTER 5
Mourning Dove 36

CHAPTER 6
Bobwhite Quail 48

CHAPTER 7
Squirrel 52

CHAPTER 8
Ringnecked Pheasant 63

CHAPTER 9
Wild Turkey 74

CHAPTER 10
The Gun and Its Use 85

Introduction

IT'S MORE THAN 40 years since I shot my first piece of upland game, a cottontail rabbit, and I've hunted at every opportunity during every season since, except for 3 years during World War II when I was in the Army. Even then, on rare occasions, I had a few hours to hunt. Most of that was for the small roe deer of northern Europe, particularly Germany, so it wasn't upland game but it was hunting, and it was a welcome relief from the more serious hunting and shooting of that period. I mention this because I think that 40-some years of experience means I've paid my dues in this business, and this qualifies me to voice some opinions—even if the "voice" is a typewriter. (At least my old typer is an L.C. Smith; maybe there's something significant there.)

This certainly doesn't mean I know all the answers about upland hunting. I learn something new every day I spend outdoors; almost every time I talk to another hunter, no matter if he's a rank beginner or a graybeard like me; every time I read a hunting book or article—and God knows I've read enough in my lifetime, and profited from the good stuff and even the bad. I wish I could sort it out well enough to give specific credit for all the bits and pieces, but after decades of reading and talking and writing and thinking and even of studying, it's all so interwoven in my mind that it's impossible to know just where some particular item came from. Maybe at this point it doesn't matter anymore. Nevertheless, I'd like all my hunting friends who might read this—and those who will never have the chance—to know how much I appreciate the days we spent together in the briars and the other thick places. What they taught me and what we learned together are important to me, and hopefully some of it will be helpful to you. As I said a few lines back, I don't pretend to know it all, so it's highly likely that your experiences with a given bird or animal will be different to some extent, and that your solutions to certain problems will be different. No matter. There's more than one way to skin a squirrel and so long as the job gets done, that's all that matters.

I told you I've been hunting for more than 40 years. That's a big percentage of anyone's life. But I've been shooting far longer. Ever since my fourth birthday, which is now almost a half-century ago, when my father gave me a Daisy air rifle as a gift. I couldn't even cock it, of course, but he did that for me, thousands of times. Two years later my birthday present was a Crosman pellet gun, then came a Winchester .22 and a 20-gauge Remington M17, and my high school graduation present, shortly after my 17th birthday, was a M-71 Winchester .348. "That's quite a gun for a boy, but you may be quite a boy for your age," Bob Nichols told me. I don't know how true the second half of his comment was, but I do know I wanted that .348 so bad I could taste it. I still have it and wouldn't part with it under any conceivable circumstance There were other guns before that M71 and nobody knows how many since, and God willing there will be more in the years to come. I mention this in case you wonder, when you get to the gun chapter, whether the opinions have any value. Again, they're not the final answer, but what I write is based on a lot of firsthand experience as well as what others have learned and passed on, so it might be helpful if you need any help.

The second reason I mention the gun stuff here is that what I knew about guns, and could do with them, was—and is—highly important in my life. A few months after I got that .348, I was in the Army, and before I got out I'd had combat duty in France and Belgium and Holland and Luxembourg and Germany, and there were a few occasions when shooting ability made the difference between coming home alive or not. Nobody really learns gun handling in a few weeks of basic training—we spent more time polishing our boots than in shooting—as it takes time, possibly years, of living with guns to make their use an instinctive reaction to an unexpected stimulus. The reaction of such a shooter might be only a fifth-of-a-second faster than the next man's, but in a serious situation a fifth-of-a-second is a helluva long time—and can be the difference between the quick and the dead. I realize that's a melodramatic statement, but things being what they are in this world, you might be involved in such a situation some day. If you are, I hope you survive it, and maybe later you'll somehow recall that "that ol' SOB Bell knew what he was talkin' about." Even if you never get into anything so serious (most people never do and I certainly hope you don't), a few minutes of daily gun handling will make you so deadly on upland game that your buddies will feel left out of things when the birds start flushing.

Anyhow, this is a book about upland game hunting. At least it's supposed to be. When you get right down to it, there's some question about what critters belong in the upland game category. Grouse, woodcock, pheasants—of course. But turkeys? Who's to say? In the end, for reasons of my own, I included the species I wanted to and left out others—the western quail, for instance, which one friend thought should be covered. Because a number of different ones are included, and space is limited, it was impossible to go into extreme detail on any. That's just as well. In a previous book, *Hunting the Long-Tailed Bird*, I probably told readers a lot more than most of them wanted to know about the ring-necked pheasant. But at least it's there for those who want it.

This is enough of an introduction. I hope you find something interesting and helpful on the pages that follow.

Good hunting.

CHAPTER 1

Ruffed Grouse

THE RUFFED GROUSE IS king of upland birds. There's no doubt of that. There is some question whether he's acquired this ranking through recognition of his inherent qualities, which are many, or by virtue of the paeans published in his honor through the years—countless stories and articles in all the outdoor magazines, plus classic volumes such as Burton Spiller's *Grouse Feathers,* George Bird Evans's *The Upland Shooting Life,* and, most unforgettable of all, William Harndon Foster's *New England Grouse Shooting.* Books like these have lifted the grouse out of his favorite grapevine tangles and deposited him on a pedestal where generations of upland hunters have come to worship. I'm not saying such veneration is completely uncalled for—the grouse is a truly great game bird—yet there are times when all the hoopla, the super-bird mystique, does seem a bit much. I've got a feeling that if anyone discussed the whole thing with the grouse, his reaction would be dignified embarrassment. There can be too much of a good thing.

Dignified is the word that to me best describes this bird. Sure I know about his thunderous takeoff (or his silent slipaway when it pleases him), his brilliantly executed thick-woods flights, his quiet courage when the breaks go against him. Still, when I think about grouse, which I do every now and again, it's not his explosiveness that comes in mind so much as his quiet dignity. A grouse, left to his own devices, doesn't go around showing off. I doubt he even thinks about the magic of his flight. He just does it when necessary. Mostly, I'm sure, he merely goes his own way, striding softly through the dappled woods, poised, alert, sleek looking even when actually somewhat chunky, minding his own business, the unobtrusive king of his domain.

Maybe it's this reserve, this lack of brashness, combined with his quiet unassuming colors, that has made so many fine outdoor writers take up the drums in his behalf. Knowing through personal experience what an outstanding game bird he is, they're bothered because he simply doesn't proclaim, "I am the greatest." So they do it for him—with the best of intentions no doubt, but perhaps not recognizing that in addition to his other virtues the grouse is a truly modest creature who would far prefer to be left alone.

Most of us, when we think of grouse hunting, think of New England. There's something about that stern region, its ancient rocky hills, dark woods, hidden swamps, sometimes pierced by a shaft of sunlight that transforms a glen into a cathedral, that's simply home for the grouse. Yet the grouse is native to vast tracts of the North American continent. He's found as far north as central Alaska, down and across much of Canada, from the rain forests of British Columbia to the mixed hardwood-conifers at the edge of the Atlantic. In the contiguous states, he's at home in the forested regions from the Pacific Northwest through the Great Lakes states to Maine, in the wooded highlands of our south-central states and in the Appalachians south to Georgia. Wildlife biologists recognize a variety of subspecies—eight or 10—scattered across the continent, and undoubtedly they have valid reasons for the differentiation. But most hunters are unimpressed by such technicalities. If they ever ponder a scientific name at all, it's *Bonasa umbellus* that comes to mind, the Latin term for the accepted basic species. Few of us would even recognize that if it weren't mentioned occasionally in popular

Sam Slaymaker pauses at the end of a hunt to recall what a great day it was. This time he even has a pair of grouse to show for it, and such tangibles don't come every time.

writing, so there's little point in going into the variations. They're minor anyway. The bird itself is pretty much the same, along the Yukon River in Alaska or in the damp grapevine hollows of Pennsylvania. It has far more popular names than scientific ones—these things tend to vary with locality—but "partridge" and "mountain pheasant" seem the most common after just plain "grouse." When I was growing up in east-central Pennsylvania, a couple of uncles always corrupted the named into "ruffled grouch," which seemed a bit comic to me even at the time, though I never laughed when I heard it. Old Irishmen don't take kindly to being laughed at by kids. This term of course comes close to describing a typical grouse hunter after a miss, so maybe it ties in all right anyway.

Grouse Habits and Habitat

As with many other species, male grouse have a strong sense of territory—an area they regard as their own. They declare this by drumming—rapidly flexing the wings while standing erect, usually on a "drumming log," with the spread tail used as a brace, ruff and head crest extended. The sound produced is distinctive, at first a slow thud that brings to mind the one-lunger gasoline engines used on various small Susquehanna River boats when I was a kid. It rapidly increases to a roar, then slows to a stop. There have been numerous explanations for the way the sound is produced, but it is currently accepted that it is caused by air rushing into a partial vacuum caused by the rapidly beating wings, the feathers of which are spread during this act.

It's often difficult to pinpoint a drumming grouse. The sound runs along ridges or through valleys in a remarkable manner, sometimes sounding close when it's far away, or far when it's near. I had an unusual example of this some years ago. I was moose hunting in Ontario one October and about midmorning sat down on an old log in heavy, shadowy cover, intending to eat a sandwich. Before I got it unwrapped, I heard a distant drumroll, so muted that I felt certain the bird was a mile or more away. I didn't pay the slightest attention when it sounded several more times. But finally, in a sort of reluctant response to the persistent sound, I looked back to

Three cottontails, a pair of grouse and one black squirrel make a mixed bag that any upland hunter would be proud of.

my right, along the length of the log. There at the far end, which was scarcely 15 feet from me, was the grouse, drumming like crazy, those stubby wings just a blur in the dark woods. I don't know what he thought I was—an intruder on his turf, perhaps, though this was fall and not the spring breeding season—but he didn't seem in the least bit frightened of me. He did fly when I stood up, but I'm not sure it was through fear. He probably just didn't want to be near anything as strange as a moose hunter.

Drumming can take place anytime during the year, but usually it is concentrated in spring. Only the males do it. Besides staking out a territory, drumming undoubtedly has sexual connotations, if not attracting a female at least making her aware of the male's presence and warning other cockbirds of the drummer's existence and location. Males often fight at this time of the year when one wanders into another's area. Hens pay little attention to drumming, so the male takes to

Wayne Kober gets ready for a cup of coffee while the dogs and Chuck Fergus look at a bird Greg Grabowicz killed. One grouse might not seem like much to show for a full day's hunt by four men and a pair of Labs (the author was behind the camera), but everyone concerned was satisfied with the results. It's easy to have worse days.

(Above) "There comes a pause in the day's occupation, that's known as . . . " What? The time to solidify some memories so they can be called back in the years to come when the hills are too steep? Maybe. Some days are easier than others to remember of course, and this looks like one of those.

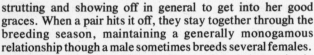

(Right) When a grouse hunter gets this lucky, it serves to create a reminder that the king of upland game can be successfully pursued and brought to bag.

strutting and showing off in general to get into her good graces. When a pair hits it off, they stay together through the breeding season, maintaining a generally monogamous relationship though a male sometimes breeds several females.

A grouse nest is not an impressive creation. A depression in the leaves, usually in a wooded area and backed up against the base of a tree or a log, just about says it all. The mated hen faces outward, apparently liking the feeling of security the solid "wall" behind her gives. A clutch of six to 16 eggs is normal and incubation takes about 24 days. The male takes no part in this. Fertility is high, and renesting occurs if something happens to the first clutch early in the incubation.

Baby grouse are precocial and develop rapidly. Nevertheless, growing up is not an easy chore. It isn't unusual for half of a clutch to die from low temperatures or wetness during their first weeks, even though the hen tries to protect them beneath her at night. On occasion, the hen will also attack predators to save her chicks, or fool a predator into following her as she puts on the broken-wing trick.

Insects are the important food item for chicks, their high protein level making for rapid growth. By 3 weeks the young birds are flying some, and in another 3 weeks they have their juvenile plumage.

In summer, life is relatively easy for grouse. There's always some predator problem—most wild creatures live with that constantly—but the weather is easy, there's plenty of food, and the young birds are getting bigger every day. As soon as they can fly reasonably well, at 3 to 4 weeks of age, they can avoid many predators simply by flying away during the daytime and roosting in trees at night. Thus, though these birds spend most of their time on the ground, the magic of flight is often a very practical answer to various problems.

During warm weather, grouse loaf around, eat when they feel like it, take dust baths to control parasites such as the ticks, fleas and lice which are common at this time of year, and in general take things easy. In midsummer the adults go into their annual molt. Most of the primary wing feathers are lost

at one time, so they cannot fly, which must be a traumatic experience for such a bird.

In early fall, brood breakup takes place and the young birds scatter to find living areas of their own. Apparently there is no plan for this, but merely an instinct to disperse. This results in the so-called crazy flights, when young grouse take off in random directions, appear in suburbs, and so on. Eventually things get straightened out and by the time hunting season rolls around, grouse activities have pretty much reverted to normal.

Knowing what a game bird eats can help a hunter to find it during the open season or understand it better in general, so it pays to give some thought to the grouse's diet. Though chicks eat insects almost exclusively, adult birds depend primarily on plant foods except in summer when they too devour many caterpillars, beetles, and whatever else in the bug line they can find. Aspens are a favored food, both the buds and the leaves, and at various times of the year so are blackberries, thornapples, raspberries, strawberries, birch buds, cherry buds and fruit, apple buds, ironwood and hazel catkins, chokeberry, dogwood, beechnuts, acorns, clover and laurel leaves. This list does not exhaust the grouse's food possibilities—it's known to feed on more than 500 kinds of plants—but does give some idea of his diet.

Cover also is vital to grouse. They are not birds of the farmlands as pheasants are, except possibly reverting farms of the more remote and hilly regions. At least they're not commonly found in areas of intense cultivation. Nor are they birds of mature forests, where large high trees shade out the brush and undergrowth, leaving little for any huntable species of wildlife to subsist on. Rather, it is the logged-off forest areas which have grown up to brush that support good grouse populations. These provide food, protection during the breeding and young-raising times, and some protection against the wind and the cold of winter. Chopped off or burned areas quickly produce good sprout growth; greenbriars and mountain laurel thickets are great; thick pine stands, abandoned orchards, occasional wild crab apple trees near old woods roads, grapevine-grown ravines, woods edges which have been cut back along fields to reduce shading, osage orange thickets, aspen and witch hazel stands, juneberry clumps—these are the kinds of things which provide cover and other necessities for grouse. Where they exist, whatever grouse are in the area will be found.

Grouse Population and Survival

Sometimes, of course, there are no grouse—or very few—in a given area, no matter what the food and cover. Populations seem to be cyclic, fluctuating up and down, from periods of almost excess to periods of almost non-existence, in something resembling a predictable pattern. We say "resembling" because no one seems truly capable of explaining such a pattern of change, and a few observers argue that such cycles simply don't exist. At any rate, in a given time and place, grouse may not be found, even though there seems to be no ready explanation for their absence. Local scarcity can be a result of a cold wet spring coming on the heels of a bad winter. Weather like this kills not only the chicks, which are highly susceptible to such conditions, but also the hens in many cases, as they try to protect their young. Eggs and chicks can also be destroyed by snakes, skunks, raccoons, opossums, crows, stray house cats and other hungry critters. Even if chicks survive to adulthood, they still face the dangers

With his open-bored SKB 12-gauge ready, the author moves along an old woods road on a wet morning. Grouse are often flushed near such roads, but fast shooting is needed to down one. Old pigskin shirt and heavy canvas pants made for construction work provide protection in the thick cover.

Don Lewis takes a moment to admire the bird he's downed. As a real hunter, he recognizes the grouse as a wonderful game species that deserves respect and maybe even a touch of love. It's hard for a non-hunter to believe this relationship exists, but most true hunters know it does.

of predation and accidental death. Road-killed grouse are not uncommon in mountainous areas cut by highways, and of course owls, hawks, foxes, coyotes and other predators must eat to survive. There's nothing unusual or wrong about this: One creature has as much right to live as the next. Nevertheless, there are times when the overall effect on the grouse population is depression.

By fall, grouse are usually living as scattered individuals, though occasionally concentrations of them are noted. Food is still plentiful and most birds reach their maximum weight now. Fall is also the time of the hunter, and we'll go into that shortly. Meanwhile, let's take a short look at the grouse in winter.

When the weather turns miserable, with low temperatures, howling winds and deep snow, many winged creatures point themselves south and just fly away from it all. That's a great solution to this season's problems, one which many humans emulate, though their wings are of man-made metal and jet fuel supplies their power. Other species, perhaps those which are innately tougher, refuse to leave. (Okay, so they're not designed for migratory flight. You know it and I know it. But somehow it's more satisfying to believe that brave tough little critters like the grouse simply refuse to leave their dark beloved covers.)

At any rate, survival in winter is not an easy thing. To maintain an acceptable metabolic condition, good quantities of food are required, for even feathered creatures radiate heat at an alarming rate when temperatures are low. Snow and ice

The thunder of a grouse flushing somewhere behind him makes Chuck Fergus pause, but on this day they were going out wild, often too far out to even be seen. Still you keep looking. If enough cover is hit, a bird will offer a shot — something that never happens if you just talk about hunting while watching the game of the week.

When snow blankets the ground and harsh winds cut through the bare trees, grouse hunters investigate every bit of thick cover, hoping to flush a bird.

commonly cover ground supplies, and food such as insects and low-growing berries are nonexistent now. Fortunately for the grouse, he is not dependent on these items, welcome as they were during warmer months. Instead of trying to scratch through deep snow cover on the remote chance of finding something edible, he simply takes to the tree and dines on high-protein buds and catkins, or winter-available leaves such as those of mountain laurel. The buds of aspen, cherry, apple and birch trees are particular favorites.

As part of the grouse's survival equipment in snow country, nature provides built-in snowshoes for the winter months. These are tiny cylindrical extensions of skin which extend outward from the midline of the toes for about 1/10-inch. They increase the surface area of the feet and make it easier for the bird to walk on soft fluffy snow. These useful growths develop in early fall and are shed in spring, another process beyond the ability of man to equal.

At this time of year all grouse are large enough to roost in trees, yet the nights are long and bitterly cold over much of their range, even when huddled in wind-breaking conifers. To survive, grouse often use the very snow which can be such a problem to other creatures. Nobody knows how or when grouse learned that they could burrow or plunge deeply into soft snow and ignore the below-zero temperatures that enveloped winter's black north woods, but somehow they learned. Dry snow is full of dead air, and dead air is an excellent insulator, and grouse take advantage of this by diving from the air or a tree into deep drifts, or by planting

themselves belly down on the surface and quickly shimmying their way downward, almost supernaturally disappearing as the dry white stuff settles itself on top of them. If the drift is deep enough, a grouse might go several feet beneath the surface. There, his body heat, trapped by the snow's insulation, will raise the temperature of his cubbyhole to almost the freezing level. If this still sounds chilly, stop and remember that his feathers provide perfect comfort at that level—and on top of the snow the temperature might be 30 below! When drifts aren't deep enough for this method, grouse sometimes just squat down in a place that suits their instinct and let falling snow cover them completely. This probably isn't as warm a situation as the deep hole—there's less insulation—but it can well mean the difference between surviving and perishing. In the end, that's all that matters to a wild creature.

Plumage and Sex Determination

As Einstein or someone once said, everything is relative. Thus, to a quail or dove shooter, grouse are large birds, while to a confirmed pheasant hunter they're more in the medium class, and to a goose or turkey hunter, whose targets may reach 15 to 25 pounds, grouse are small. Considering his range overall, it takes a pretty big grouse to register 1½ pounds on a scale, which is about half the size of an adult wild ringneck. A longtime friend of mine, the late Paul Failor, as part of his job while employed by the Pennsylvania Game Commission, had occasion to weigh a good number of grouse taken on the ridge country bordering southeastern Pennsylvania's most fertile farming region. The heaviest he ever weighed there went 2¼ pounds, with the average adult going to 1½ to 1¾ pounds and a fall-killed bird of the year about 1¼ pounds. Most of the grouse's weight seems concentrated in the breast, delicious white meat that will please anyone—gourmet or hungry hunter—when properly prepared.

The grouse has a wingspread of approximately 2 feet and a length of 16 to 19 inches, including the squared-off tail which the male can fan out into a perfect semicircle. (The female can spread her tail feathers in a similar fashion, but usually the feathers will not overlap at the edges when this is done; this is one way of determining whether a bird is male or female.) Grouse feathers are a rich brown color, not gaudy in any sense, with a sprinkling of black and white on top. The breast feathers are an off white, darker on the male, with horizontal dark brown bars which are interrupted on the female. The tail is mostly brown. Near the tail's end is a fairly wide band, nearly black in color, between narrower gray-brown bands. On male birds, this dark band is normally (though not always) unbroken, while on females the two central feathers of the band commonly have a sort of speckled brown-black appearance. This feature helps to "sex" birds in the field, as do the lengths of the tail feathers. Central tail feathers longer than 5¼ inches, measured from the body, unplucked, or over 5⅞ inches including the full shaft, indicate the bird is probably a male. Tail feathers of females are shorter.

The grouse's wings are short and rounded, excellent for maneuvering through thick cover. They, too, can be helpful in determining sex and age as the tips of the leading primaries on young birds are pointed, while those of older birds have become rounded off.

Two Canadian wildlife biologists, Yvon Rousell and Reginald Ouellet, have come up with yet another telltale feather marking, in regard to sexing, what might be called the rump-feather technique. In this method, feathers on the bird's back, near the tail but not adjacent to it, show different patterns on males and females: whitish spots near the tips of the rump feathers. A single white spot indicates the bird is a female, while two or three such spots indicate it's a male. This method is, in itself, not foolproof, as occasionally some rump feathers on a given male may have but one dot. However, when used in conjunction with other identification techniques it is very helpful.

The ruffed grouse gets his name from the ruff of feathers that form epaulets on the female, sometimes a collar on the male. These are usually nearly black in color, with iridescent highlights, though occasionally a chocolate-colored ruff is encountered. This occurs in a red color phase of this species, these birds having rusty feathers and dark-brown tail band. Another color variation is the so-called "silvertail," which has gray rather than brown in the tail.

The previous paragraphs have quite a bit of material on sexing and aging grouse, subjects which might not interest everyone at first. Yet they are important in the overall picture. It's easy to differentiate between the sexes of some game birds—enough so that regulations can restrict hunting to male pheasants, for instance, if this is felt necessary—but difficult with others. A few friends say they can pick out male bobwhites when a covey flushes, and Roger Latham, outdoor editor of the *Pittsburgh Press,* tells me he oftentimes differentiates between males and females when grouse flush, usually by recognizing the longer tail of the male. Such experts shoot only cockbirds, leaving the females to breed. Most hunters never reach such a state of efficiency—they're usually thankful just to hit any flushing quail or grouse—but at least if they can sex and age a bird after it's in the hand, the information can be valuable when wildlife researchers collect such data through hunting surveys. The information gives them some idea of the age structure of the population, the reproductive rate, etc.

Cover

Hunting, of course, is what this is all about. Most hunters are interested in the game birds and animals they pursue, but their interest is not merely academic. They tend to use their knowledge not only to satisfy certain intellectual urges but also to help them hunt game, find it and make it table fare.

I've been hunting grouse, when conditions wherever I lived made it feasible, since the late '30s. That's four decades now, less a few years spent in the Army during World War II, when the shooting was of the more serious kind. I don't believe that makes me an expert grouse hunter by any means. It would be nice to think otherwise, but it's better to face facts. So far as that goes, I'm not sure there are any experts any more, which makes it easier to live with my own inadequacies.

For best success with grouse, you should hunt them where they are. That seems so obvious it shouldn't require mention, but a lot of young hunters don't realize it and waste much of their available time looking for these square-tailed birds where they rarely exist. I wouldn't say grouse are never found in the flat weedfields of traditional farm country, say, but it's highly unlikely. (Some years ago I might have said never, but then I killed a grouse in exactly such a situation in southeastern Pennsylvania pheasant country, literally miles from typical grouse cover, which once more proves that it doesn't pay to be dogmatic when speaking of any kind of wildlife.)

Typical grouse cover includes reverting mountain farmland, particularly around old apple orchards, bramble patches, cut-over areas, alder runs, grapevine-strangled hollows, blowdowns interspersed with berry vines, slightly swampy wood patches, old overgrown stone walls and other places where thick cover predominates. They also are found in small woodlots, along the edges of larger forests, near small openings where a large tree has fallen in the woods, in the vicinity of ancient leaf-covered tote roads, and so on.

Such spots offer the food and cover grouse like, and almost always they provide immediate vanishing possibilities for this fast-flushing fellow. Any gunner who is going to have regular success on grouse (which doesn't mean hitting every bird, but perhaps one in three) has to be a good gun handler, one with iron nerves and fast reactions. It's not that a grouse actually flushes so fast or that he's so far away. Most are within easy range when they take off and scientific types who dote on such things insist that his flushing speed is on the order of 25 mph, which is not very fast at all, viewed objectively. The big problem is the noise he makes when leaving. His typical departure is a roaring blast-off that tends to freeze the gunner's senses and physical reactions, turning his bragged-on fluidlike follow-through into something resembling a spoon being shoved through Jello, flat side first. Few hunters remain objective when that roar fills their eardrums. There's a tendency to freeze—probably dating back to an instinct from the mists of our past when, to avoid being seen when a sudden danger appeared, our ancestors repressed all motion while their eyes and other senses frantically searched for the source of the threat. It takes only a second or two to recognize that the flushing roar is coming from a grouse—the objective of our hunt—and another half-second to get off a shot. But when we give Ol' Ruff a couple of seconds to depart unmolested—he's gone! In his usual dense cover, he has to go only a short distance to get out of sight. And he has a fantastic ability to bend and twist around trees and brush and vines, boring through holes in the shrubbery like a bullet going down a barrel. To say he puts on a great exhibit of flying skill is an understatement . . . all of which is one reason so many gunners are so fond of him.

Guns, Dogs and Hunting Technique

The way to hit grouse, of course, is to not let yourself be flustered by his takeoff but rather to use the noise as a stimulus to which you react by swinging the gun through the path of the departing bird and firing.

Having a good grouse dog can take some of the pressure off insofar as the roaring takeoff goes . . . or possibly build it up for the kind of hunter who becomes nervous when moving up to a pointing setter and anticipating a flush within seconds. Personally, I'd sooner take my chances with a bird I flush myself, reacting to the noise, than to deliberately boot one out ahead of the dog. But I'm probably in the minority in this. I should point out that here I'm referring to shooting only, and don't mean to downgrade the tremendous satisfaction that comes from hunting with a fine dog. There are all sorts of rewards in this besides the normal improvement in hitting.

Good grouse dogs are scarce in my part of the world. Maybe everywhere. But the guys who know say that it's important to get a dog that has a good nose, a strong desire to hunt and intelligence. And then train him on grouse. It takes time, but the dog must learn through experience where birds most likely will be found, that he must approach them from downwind, point the moment he catches scent, and cautiously follow a moving bird without flushing it. Grouse, as with many wild creatures, are easily disturbed by the human voice, so the dog should work well without a lot of vocal instructions. And it helps immeasurably if he's a top-notch retriever. A wounded grouse will run or crawl or burrow into the tightest cover where a man has almost no chance of finding it; here, a good dog literally means the difference between success and failure of a shot that crippled.

Insofar as the shooting itself goes, the basic requirements are a fast-handling, open-bored gun, preferably one that's short enough to swing easily in the thick stuff, with 1 to 1⅛ ounces of 7½ shot. Chances usually are short, around 18-25 yards on average, though in the woods they tend to seem longer because the light is poor. Some hunters use 8s or 9s, and these give very dense patterns that can be deadly at short range because they increase your chances of a head shot. They make a fine choice for the open barrel of a double, but if I had to choose only one size for grouse, it would be 7½s. Many times the extra penetration is needed—a 1½-pound bird is not really a tiny thing like a quail—and 7½s seem more dependable in leafy cover.

Every bird shot at should be searched for if there's any likelihood it was hit. Dense cover often prevents seeing the bird at the moment of firing—sometimes the shot is let off when the bird is actually invisible—so you don't always see whatever reaction might indicate a hit. Stand motionless after firing, if the bird has vanished, and listen intently. Commonly, you'll hear the thump of the grouse hitting the forest floor. Get to it quickly, in case it's a runner. Even if you don't hear any such thing, follow the flight direction a ways, looking carefully for any indication that you connected. Sometimes a feather will be seen wafting downward, sometimes the reflexive drumming of wings against the leaf covered ground will lead you to a dead bird, and sometimes, if you go a reasonable ways, you'll reflush the bird you missed. Regardless, make a search after every shot. It's good for both your conscience and the dinner table.

I remember several grouse shots which are pleasant to bring to mind on long winter evenings when the fire is low and a storm presses the den's window but I know I'm safe and warm inside. I'll talk about them because they're typical. None is of my first grouse. I was young when I bagged him, maybe 13, and that whole thing's a blur. It was just a blur at the moment of the shot, and it'll never change now, but I remember some others well.

The first I want to mention occurred in 1950, in a narrow thickly grown ravine running up from Little Fishing Creek, in central Pennsylvania. I was only a few hundred yards from home, moving up through the damp bottom, hoping to kick out a rabbit or a pheasant and wondering if I could get the safety off in time if I should move game. I was carrying a Sauer drilling I'd liberated in Germany a few years earlier, and its safety, on the left side of the pistol grip, was almost flush with the surface of the stock. I don't know who designed that item but it wasn't made for fast shooting and I altered it shortly afterward. I wasn't expecting a grouse as they were infrequently seen in that area, but one went out suddenly (is there any other way?) and I found myself frantically thumbing for that flat-headed safety even as I flipped the Sauer around. Wiping it through the head-high willows, my gaze somehow fastening on a brown streak that was rapidly reaching a vanishing point among some sumac just above. The drilling was muzzle heavy, an advantage to the swing once I got it moving, and just as the buttplate hit my shoulder my finger hit the trigger. There was a streak of exploding brush that terminated in a puff of feathers and a dead bird hanging motionless for a moment in midair. It wasn't a particularly unusual grouse

The bird was there, but he's gone now. Sometimes even a fast-reacting gunner is too late, and nobody would want it otherwise. There's nothing wrong with the bird winning.

Until the early '50s, autoloaders were not legal for hunting in Pennsylvania, so countless shooters who grew up with slide actions still prefer them. John Kriz is one such hunter. He can shuck 'em out as fast as an auto and never has to worry that the action won't work because of a defective shell or whatever.

Neither of these shots was unusual either, not for any grouse hunter, but always in the minds of people like us, they're minor miracles in their own right, with a life of their own. That of course is reason enough for describing these two shots, but there's a more pedestrian purpose and it's simply this: Grouse can be in any tiny bit of cover if the conditions are right, so a hunter should remember this and be expecting one to flush, even when a flush is unlikely. And when a bird appears, he should shoot—right now—instead of pondering the unexpected fact while the game makes its escape. After all, that's what a hunter is out there for.

The last grouse I shot deserves mention. It was a gloomy, misty day, in a corner of deep woods on a ridge paralleling

Sometimes the dog thinks he oughta have a bird for himself — at least til he's had a chance to snuff it good. That's why Nick Sisley isn't taking him seriously.

shot. In fact, it was almost typical—which is to say it somehow gave the impression of being nearly impossible—and that's probably why I remember it after all these years.

A couple of seasons later, Dad and I were hunting pheasants on a farm near home. After working some fields, we got into a thick sidehill, part of which had been cut off. Brown-leaved oak tops lay scattered through a mixture of brambles, sumac, honeysuckle, stumps, weeds, and small logs that had been cut but never dragged out. All in all it was quite a mess, the sort of place you're likely to find most anything. Again, I was thinking of rabbits or roosters, simply because we weren't in good grouse country. But a sudden roar brought me swinging around just in time to see one of these brown buzzbombs flashing right across my front, no more than 12 yards away. I never paused, I never thought, I just swung the Sweet Sixteen as fast and as hard as I could, slapping the trigger even as the bird disappeared behind a small standing cedar—and watching a ball of puffing feathers come out of the far side.

"Great!" Dad yelled, and then, before I had time to lower the little Browning, another grouse slanted away in the opposite direction, coming out of the jungle where the first one had thumped down. Again without thinking, I reversed the path of my barrel, swinging with all my might, and there was a distant *boom* and a second brown bird tumbled down from the air, almost as if I had some godlike power to simply point my finger and end its days...and in so doing make it a part of the memories that I'll treasure till my own life is gone.

When the sun begins to droop in the west after a long cold day in the woods, it's good to know a scalding shower and a hot meal are waiting . . . and it's even better to know your legs were equal to the steep slippery hills and your gun to the wild flushing birds, for such days tie you to your hunting ancestors of ages past.

Pennsylvania's famed Cumberland Valley. Three of us had been out a couple of hours, had hunted hard, but hadn't fired a shot. That's not unusual. Grouse hunting is in many respects similar to following bear tracks in the snow—a lot of exercise, usually with little to show for it at the end. But we kept going, as you always do as long as daylight holds.

We were angling through a narrow stand of conifers, not really expecting anything there, hoping the next stretch would be better. It was fairly open as many of the lower branches had died, but dark as a cave with the rain filtering down through the high crowns and silent underfoot because of the thick layer of shed needles. I was on the right end of our line, squinting ahead toward the edge of a field where the sky showed lighter gray, when I sensed a flash of movement to my right. My head snapped around just in time to see a grouse leveling off a few feet off the ground after silently diving almost vertically from a high limb to squirt away to my rear as if blasted out of a bazooka. I'm not sure how I got turned around, but I did. It was a purely reflexive action, with no thought at all, the kind of response that bypasses the brain and brings instantaneous movement. Even as I swung 180 degrees on the ball of my right foot, the butt of the SKB over-under was slamming against my shoulder, my left foot was ramming into the ground to stop my rotation, and somewhere in the midst of all that my finger slapped the trigger and the gun went *boom* and that speeding bird puffed up half again its size and then thudded into the ground. I'll never forget that moment. It was the kind of shot that ordinary gunners like me make only a few times in their lives, and that's why I'm writing about it. There are times when it's good to know you did the impossible.

Just one more example, because it too was a typical chance, and we'll wrap up this chapter on the King.

I was hunting alone, as I've done much of my life, and again was working up through the ravine mentioned a few paragraphs back. This time, though, I was carrying the Browning Sweet Sixteen instead of the Sauer. It was a far better grouse gun as it was bored improved cylinder rather than modified and full, and I'd altered the stock enough that it fit me perfectly. In almost the same place as the earlier shot, I flushed another grouse but it went out at an impossible angle and vanished in an instant. But I knew grouse don't often fly far, and I followed it up and managed to flush it again, and again had no shot. There are times like that, a lot of them when you take time to add them up, but I was young and persistent and

kept poking around, hoping for just one more flush. It didn't come, though I hit every possible bit of cover in that whole gut. Eventually I worked up toward the top and through some thick pines, thinking perhaps it had gone farther than expected. Still no luck.

I was mad at myself for not getting off a shot on one of the earlier flushes, though I knew that would have been impossible, and for quite awhile I hunted back and forth through the area, tromping every bit of thick cover I could get my boots into. I even circled back through the ravine. Nothing. Finally, I conceded defeat and slanted up the sidehill toward a field where I thought I might boot out a ringneck. Right at the top of the ravine, along the edge of the field, was a small patch of ankle-high brown grass, and I automatically walked through it, still mumbling to myself, and out went that crazy grouse. Straight away, angling upward at a slight angle against the wide open sky, the absolutely easiest chance I've ever had at one of these gutsy birds in a lifetime of hunting, and I flipped the gun up, knowing he was finally dead and in my gamebag, and proceeded to miss him three shots—*Boom! Boom! Boom!* —just like that.

That, too, is typical. In fact, that's the most typical result of any chance at this loveliest of game birds. And I hold that memory like a treasure deep within myself, sometimes conjuring it up when things are going bad for me as they were for that bird, for it reminds me that there are times when, no matter how great the odds are stacked against you, you can still win.

Well, I think this should make it clear I'm no great shucks as a grouse hunter. I didn't live when the fabulous numbers were available, the kind of numbers it takes to make a good grouse gunner, and I doubt that I'll be around when those numbers return. Still, it's good to know there were great grouse hunters in the earlier days. They're gone now, almost all of them; the few that are left are too old to hunt and even the memories of their legends are fading. But sometimes just at dusk, on a dim old tote road that flanks an abandoned apple orchard, I'm almost sure I see a lank, canvas-clad shadow shuffling toward the light that gleams in a farmhouse window down below. The long barrels of the old double draped over his arm catch what little sky light there is, and an old setter droops along at his heels, not tired, not frisky, just ready to go home, content with the small bulge in the back of the man's canvas coat, both of them knowing that tomorrow is another day.

I hope it's one of the guys I think it is.

CHAPTER 2

Woodcock

Five of the big-eyed longbills mean this was another good day for Nick Sisley. But he obviously knows where a lot of the credit goes.

WOODCOCK ARE CRAZY BIRDS. Maybe it's because their brains are upside down. Still, an awful lot of upland hunters, particularly those who rank the ruffed grouse as their top target, are intrigued by this chunky little long-billed fellow who flies as if he missed a few lessons when learning how. Of course, that makes him a tricky target—how can the gunner anticipate what he's going to do when the bird himself doesn't know—but going from grouse to woodcock hunting is, to my mind, the classic example of going from the sublime to the ridiculous. Nevertheless, if the old worm eater *Philohela minor* titillates your trigger finger, have at him.

Woodcock not only fly in a crazy fashion, they also look crazy. Picture a big-eyed, mottled russet, brown and beige, 6-ounce bird that's less than a foot in length, including the bill, and ponder the fact that the bill itself makes up almost 3 inches of his total length. If a pheasant had a bill of that proportion to his size, you'd need a 10-gauge autoloader stuffed with magnum loads of 2s to keep him from skewering you on opening day, just 'cause he didn't want you in his cornfields. But no one has ever accused the woodcock of being aggressive, and no one ever will. He's just a pleasant little fellow who tweets and whistles his way up and down half a continent in spring and fall, and along the way provides some great gunning for aficionados who regulate weeks of their time by his comings and goings.

The American woodcock, which is what we're considering here (there's a European cousin, *Scolopax rusticola,* which is similar in appearance but about twice as heavy), has a lot of common names, "timberdoodle," "big-eye" and "bogsucker" probably being the ones most often heard. In the Pennsylvania Dutch country a bit southeast of my home, he's occasionally referred to as "bushschnip," and we've been told that some Missourians call him "Indian hen," a term which occasional Pennsylvanians apply to the pileated woodpecker. It would be pointless to try to list all of the woodcock's local names, but it seems worth mentioning that the Old English term *wude-cocc* accounts for his non-scientific monicker. Actually, most of the hunters I've associated with always refer to this bird as "woodcock." I've often thought that names such as timberdoodle and big-eye were perpetuated more by outdoor writers striving for synonyms than by hunter' speech. No matter. A rose by any other name, etc.

The woodcock breeds across much of southern Canada as far west as Manitoba, down to Florida, Louisiana and Texas. It's a migratory critter which heads south when the weather turns cool, returning when the sun's rays heat the more northern latitudes. He usually shows up in Pennsylvania in late February or early March. The woodcock has to avoid truly cold weather for well over half of its diet is earthworms, and it can't probe for these when the ground is frozen. In addition to worms, about one-third of its food is insects, and these, too, are easier to obtain in warm weather than cold. The remainder of its diet is plant food, primarily seeds. Most feeding is done just before dawn and during early evening. The woodcock does a lot of eating, often devouring half its weight in worms in a day.

Males establish "singing grounds" in spring, small brushy areas in or near woods. Here the male gives his nasal buzz, variously described as a *peent* or *beezp,* which has an attraction for the female. A less audible *too-koo* sometimes precedes the *peent* as he struts. When properly inspired at dawn or dusk, or intending to be inspiring, the male takes off, climbs several hundred feet into the air, usually in a spiral, then zigzags downward, sounding a series of liquid chirps as he comes. If the singing ground is good size, several males often use it simultaneously. Flights last about a minute, and begin and end at the same field. The sounds made by the male, both vocal and with the wings, attract the female to the site and mating takes place. Males may mate with several females.

Woodcock are ground nesters. Nests are unimpressive—a few leaves or whatever in a small depression, usually concealed and near the edge of medium-low cover. Hawthorn, crab apple, alder, gray dogwood and aspen are favorite covers, at least in Pennsylvania. The average clutch consists of four eggs, smaller clutches tending to occur late in the season. On rare occasions five eggs may be laid. Both sexes incubate, the period being about 21 days. A nest might be abandoned if the adult is disturbed early in the incubation; in such cases, re-nesting often occurs. Later on, only extreme danger will cause abandonment. Predators such as skunks, raccoons, opossums, snakes and crows destroy some nests, but again we should realize that these creatures are only doing what comes naturally; that is, trying to survive in a world where survival is not always easy. Too often, humans condemn other predators simply because, for reasons of our own, we set a higher value on the prey species than on the predators. Viewed from the snake's position, for instance, he's doing nothing wrong. Personally, I like woodcock more than snakes, but I still can't bring myself to criticize any creature for trying to find something to eat. This attitude also applies to the hawk that sometimes eats the snake, of course.

Woodcock eggs measure about 1½ x 1¼ inches—an impressive size for such a small bird—and are gray to buff color, with reddish-brown and darker-gray markings. Chicks, which are precocial, split the shells lengthwise (perhaps unique among birds), and leave the nest within a few hours of hatching. Nesting success is high, 60-70 percent, and juvenile mortality is low. This is fortunate because only one brood per year is raised and it is not a large one. During inclement weather the hen broods her chicks until they're a few days old, but soon they're fending for themselves. In about 2 weeks they are flying and in 2 more weeks they are almost fully grown. Males attain a maximum weight of about 6 ounces, females 8. Wingspread approaches 20 inches, though that doesn't seem likely until you stretch and measure one. Besides being heavier than males, females also have longer bills, with a maximum length of about 77 millimeters, as compared with about 68 millimeters maximum for the male. The width of the leading primary wing feather can also help in differentiating between the sexes. In females it averages 3.9 millimeters wide at a point 2 centimeters from the tip; this measurement in males averages 2.8 millimeters. Seen in the air, females have a blockier appearance, at least to the hunter who sees enough of them to have more than passing familiarity with the species.

The woodcock's bill is really much more than an oddity. It's a complex development that gives this bird the ability to

Bob Parlaman likes his 20-gauge O/U for woodcock in thick cover, where fast shooting is necessary if any birds are to be taken home.

probe soft soil for the earthworms so important to its diet. Nerve endings toward the front end help the bird locate worms and an unusual arrangement of the muscles permits opening the upper bill's tip while it is underground, so that it can grasp its prey. The lower surface of this bill is rough, as is the tongue, to prevent slippage. The position of the eyes, high on the head and well back, gives good visibility even while probing for food, and the nostrils are on the upper end of the bill, near the skull, which makes breathing easy while searching for worms. The ears are between the bill and the eyes.

Such things will strike most hunters as a bit odd, but there's more to come. The woodcock's brain is perhaps even more unusual. The cerebellum, which controls coordination and balance, in the woodcock is below the rest of the brain and above the spinal column, rather than at the rear of the skull as with most birds. Some people theorize that during the woodcock's evolution the bill lengthened and the nostrils moved back, as did the eyes, forcing the brain back, too, so that the midbrain and hind-brain were forced down and a bit forward. In effect, this bird has an upside down brain . . . all because he wanted to be a better earthworm eater. Well, we told you earlier that woodcock are crazy.

Anyway, when temperatures begin to drop in the fall, woodcock begin to head south. Migration takes place at night, the birds—now called flight birds—stopping to feed and rest during the day. A hunter might find a covert that was empty yesterday has an abundance of birds today, as migrants arrive. It's natural to believe these birds came from the same place and are going to the same destination, but it ain't necessarily so. The arrival of these individuals at a given place at the same time can be simply coincidence, and when they leave their flight paths may well diverge so they end up states apart.

The most common sign of woodcock, except for the birds themselves, is the so-called whitewash they deposit on the leaves. Normal weather soon obliterates this, so finding it indicates birds are, or recently were, nearby. The sight of these chalky splashings is enough to bring a surge of adrenaline squirting through the veins of any old ridgerunner and make him check that both tubes of his old double are stocked with 8s.

Shot Size, Guns and Hunting Tips

Small targets taken at short range normally are shot with small pellets. For generations, an ounce of standard velocity 8s has been normal shotshell fodder for dedicated woodcockers. It's hard to argue with this selection. There are over 400 pellets in an ounce load, which means that even from a Skeet-bored tube you're getting a pattern which no woodcock can fly through at ordinary ranges. That assumes you're going to place that pattern somewhere on the target, of course. Shot size, pattern diameter and pellet density count for nothing if the gunner doesn't do a reasonable job of placing his shot.

Since woodcock lie well for the dog or the hunter, they usually flush close. They always flush slowly, and they never show much speed in flight. So hitting them should not be

With five woodcock on his lap and a pair of thunderbirds in his hands, Nick Sisley has plenty of reason to smile. The Red Gods were in a good mood this day.

It's hard to say if this hunter has any woodcock in his coat—they're too small to make much of a bulge—but he and this

Brittany are in typical 'cock country so chances are he's got a couple. (Photo by Earl V. Wise.)

difficult. It often is, though, because of the tight cover they prefer, the fact that they normally fly to daylight—which often requires a nearly vertical path on takeoff—and their fluttering, erratic flight. These characteristics tend to bamboozle gunners more used to pheasants or even grouse, and a common reaction is to fire the first shot too quickly, leading to either a missed bird or a shot-shredded one, and the second shot too slowly, in overcompensation for the first.

Best results come from proper gun drill. It's important to shift the feet into proper position when a 'cock flushes, even when the shot might be taken as is. The tiny time interval required to move the boots not only makes the shot easier because the target is now well within the area the muzzle easily covers, but also because it lets you recognize how slowly the bird is moving. Instead of a flush-bang shot, which can be deadly but which results in an inedible handful of feathers and mangled flesh, you realize there's plenty of time, you relax a bit and let Ol' Phil get out there a reasonable distance, and then you drop him cleanly. The whole thing adds up to a more satisfying experience. Sometimes, obviously, a shot must be taken immediately if not sooner, if there is to be any hope of connecting. Some covers require your fastest reactions, and on such chances you do your thing and hope for the best. But more times than most gunners realize, woodcock can be dropped at 25 or 30 yards rather than 8 or 10.

Woodcock guns follow the designs favored for grouse, the short-barreled, open-bored, smallbore double being the traditional choice for obvious reasons. These are easy carrying, well balanced and extremely fast to get into operation, and therefore do the job. Also, they're pleasant to look at, both at odd moments in the field and in the gun rack of an evening. While most grouse doubles are bored improved cylinder and modified, in a gun intended strictly for woodcock I'd go with a Skeet and Skeet selection. This choice is even deadlier at the ranges where woodcock are taken, and patterns are so large that even when an occasional shot is banged off before the butt is properly seated, you well can have a dead bird. Fact is, my favorite woodcock outfit is actually a Skeet gun, a 26-inch, vent-rib M600 SKB over-under chambered for 2¾-inch 20-gauge shells. This is a light gun but not so light that it bounces when it hits your shoulder and refuses to settle down for the shot—the effect you get with some of the ridiculously undernourished designs being built in Europe in response to a current mini-fad fostered by a few gunwriters. A 4½-pound gun might be worth an article in a copy-hungry gun magazine, but it's silly in woodcock or grouse cover. One of 6 to 6½ pounds has a more natural feel and moves better, doing what the shooter wants instead of waving around like a goosed broomstick when he's trying to get it into operation. If a 100-pound gal can easily carry and use a 6-pound shotgun— and I know several who do—I can't understand why any man would find one too much for him.

Doubles are not the only suitable woodcock guns, of course. The light autoloaders and pumps are favorites of many experienced hunters, and it would not be unreasonable to use a single shot for these birds. More times than not, it's one shot and done in alder country, so anyone who has a one-banger that fits him well should not feel he's overly handicapped. Also, a hunter who is reluctant to work over an expensive repeater might not find it amiss to alter a single shot's stock to get a fast-mounting gun and cut off the barrel to remove all choke, thus coming up with a near-perfect answer for these fluttery flushers without spending an awful lot of money. Keep in mind that what a gun looks like is not the main reason for using it; hitting well is the primary goal. Looks are for gun-nuts, not hunters.

A little ways back we mentioned that 8s are the favorite shot size of many woodcock hunters. That's true, and under-standable, but it doesn't mean you have to buy this size to kill these birds. In some parts of the country, 8s are comparatively scarce on dealers' shelves, whereas 7½s are common. If that's true in your bailiwick, use the 7½s. You'll never be able to tell the difference, nor will the birds. There's no point in carrying suggestions to silly extremes.

In Pennsylvania, woodcock usually come in season about the middle of October, along with grouse. This is a delightful time to be in the woods. At least it seems as if it ought to be. When you are sitting in your den on a cold winter night, feeling the dry oak logs in the fireplace overpower the December chill, October is a wonderful time to remember. No other month has its appeal. You always recall it as sharp, sparkling mornings, still a bit early for frost but with a tingle to the air, then warming later in the day. And you recall the leaves turning to scarlet on the hillsides, the colors of the staghorn sumac in the fencerows, and the odor of crushed grapes in dark quiet hollows. October is just as special in July or August. In midsummer, sprawled in the shade of the dense maples in the backyard, swigging an icy glass of lemonade as you glumly survey the oversize lawn that needs mowing again, your thoughts can't help but drift ahead a couple of months to when the oppressive heat will be gone and the alder patches will be a temporary home for a "fall of woodcock." That's a lovely phrase, isn't it? Perfectly descriptive, on several levels. I expect it, too, goes back to the early days in England, the Anglo-Saxon heritage with its simple but perfect descriptiveness, rather than the more highbrow Latin which often seems a bit removed from reality. At any rate, fall is the time of the woodcock, so far as the hunter is concerned, and in the minds of most of us, October is fall.

However, if we are going to be realistic about things, October isn't always those wine-colored days we love to recall. Sure, we get them occasionally, and their perfection is so complete that we let them color our memories forever. But the truth is, an awful lot of October days are miserable, insofar as weather goes. The opening day of the past season was a typical example. I'd seen no sign of woodcock locally, so was glad when Chuck Fergus told me he thought we'd have a reasonable chance for shooting along some creekbottoms and sidehills in Bald Eagle Valley. Now, Chuck lives outside of State College, Pennsylvania, so it's only 100 mile drive from my home to his, plus another 20 or so to the area he wanted to hunt. That's not unreasonable for any upland hunter, so the night before the season opened I threw my duffle in the back of the old Japanese Jeep, snugged the little SKB into the gun rack and headed northwest. The weather turned worse as I drove, spitting rain and growing chillier, but there was nothing I could do about that. Few of us can pick the days we're going to hunt; we simply go when we can get the time.

When I crawled out of the Jeep, the clouds were running fast and dark against the sky. I felt a couple drops of rain, and the wind had an edge to it. "It's gonna be a wet one," Chuck said, helping me lug my stuff in, and I agreed. Soon we were eating chili, and then we were sprawled in front of his fire, talking guns and dogs and hunting while we sipped a Scotch or two. Then it was time to hit the sack, and I spread my light down bag on the big couch in front of the fireplace, rather than taking the spare bedroom. Once or twice during the night I half woke up to watch the slow flicker of shadows from the dying fire and listen to the rain pounding against the windows.

The morning was wet. It rained only occasionally as we headed out of town, the wipers on Chuck's pickup clearing the windshield when necessary, but it had come down all night and everything was soaked. Rain gear seemed a logical choice, but neither of us bothered with it. The thing is, anytime you wear something waterproof while hunting upland

(Below) Sometimes a hunter gets lucky and bounces a 'cock out in low cover like this, but it's more likely in the higher stuff beyond.

(Above) Jim Bashline, outdoor editor of the *Philadelphia Inquirer* and associate editor of *Field & Stream* pauses to talk to Sam during a north-country hunt for long-billed birds. An outstanding dog like Sam makes finding downed birds easy.

(Left) The time always comes, whether you're ready or not, to unload the little gun and go home. By now even the dog is tired. But it was a good day.

game, which requires a lot of physical exertion, you're soon as wet from perspiration condensing inside of it as you are from the rain. It's the same with boots as with clothing. Rubber boots keep your feet dry as long as you don't wade a creek that's too deep and your feet don't sweat too much. However, when the brush is soaking wet, your pants soon are too, and then the water runs down your legs and into the boots and you're slopping along just as if you were wearing leather. So that's what I do in the first place, primarily because I find leather boots much easier to walk in and far more comfortable than rubber. Wool underwear and socks are necessary with this approach, as they're warm even when wet. The weather usually isn't extremely cold at this time of year, so a hunter wearing his usual brush clothing over wool can be comfortable enough so long as he keeps moving.

I almost got thoroughly wet before we were fully started. The first spot Chuck wanted to hunt was on the far side of a good size creek, and the approach he led me to consisted of a small elm tree which had fallen across the water when the current undercut its roots. Chuck is half my age and a good athlete, and he ambled across that skinny swaying makeshift bridge with a nonchalance stemming from numerous previous trips. I was tempted to say the hell with it and just wade the creek to begin with, but there's always a touch of challenge in stuff like this, so I put one boot in front of the other and somehow made it.

We were soon in good cover, a boggy bottom that was head high in various kinds of brush, occasional mature trees, and slashings here and there. Some distance back from the creek, the terrain slanted upward toward a wooded ridge and thornapples grew on what had once been an open sidehill. It looked like a place that ought to have some woodcock. But it didn't.

We covered the area thoroughly, our canvas clothes soon waterlogged from the wet brush, drops of water condensing on our faces and eyelashes from the misty rain that came and went through the morning, but nothing flew. By the time we'd worked through the whole cover and reached the creek a fair distance from where we'd crossed it, we saw no reason to look for another downed tree. We simply walked through the calf-high water to the far side.

"Let's try the hollow above the road, near where we parked the truck," Chuck said. "Maybe it's just too wet for them in the bottoms."

I blew a raindrop off the end of my nose and nodded. We skirted a field, half-heartedly hit some cover paralleling the old road, and headed back. As we passed the truck I caught a glimpse of my reflection in a window. I looked like a drowned rat. "Cleveland Amory should see us now," I muttered, "while we're out here enjoyin' ourselves so much killin' all these defenseless birds."

The hollow was clogged with sumac, high brush and a few dying apple trees that made small openings in the cover. We zigzagged up through it, roughly parallel, without flushing anything, then angled over one edge toward a flat that led to another wooded ridge. The cover was dense and dripping, but that was all forgotten in an instant when an explosive roar came from the far side of a downed apple tree.

"Grouse!" Chuck yelled.

I was already swinging the little SKB to cover the sound, but that's all the good it did me. The bird hadn't been 10 steps ahead of me when it flushed, but I never got a glimpse of it.

We'd had no killing frosts yet and all the trees were fully leafed. On a sunny day, the scarlets, russets and yellows would have been beautiful, but now they were just a soft soggy wall that concealed everything that was more than a few steps distant. I muttered something unprintable and angled off in the general direction the sound had gone, but with no luck.

In the next couple of hours, we had nine grouse flushes, all of them close, but I never saw a bird. Chuck had a shot but missed—just a glimpse of a sharp-angling bird that was gone before it actually registered on his mind—so I didn't get excited when he fired again a few minutes later. I hadn't heard anything, but the roar isn't an absolute prerequisite to a flush.

"Did you hit him?" I yelled, after a few moments of silence.

"Yeah. Haven't found him yet, though."

I worked toward his voice, intending to help in the search. Just as I spotted him, he leaned down and picked up a small long-billed bird.

"Funny lookin' grouse," I said.

"Yeah. But this is what we started out hunting, isn't it?"

"Come to think of it, I guess it is."

As it turned out, that woodcock was the only thing that kept us from getting skunked that day. If viewed as the total tangible reward for a lot of cold, wet hours in the brush, its value had to be considerable. Of course, it wasn't the only reason we were out there. Any day in the uplands has a value that can't be reckoned in material items such as the birds dropped, the salable photos taken, the notes that might later be incorporated into an article, but rather is something that is felt rather than seen, a sense of being part of a certain environment, an awareness that here is where you belong and that what you are doing is what you were born to do. It isn't always necessary to be a killer. It is necessary to be a hunter.

It's a bit strange that one little woodcock can bring such thoughts into the minds of an old gunner like me. In all honesty I can say that I'm not much of a woodcock killer. It's not that they're hard to hit. As mentioned, they take off slowly, fly slowly if erratically, and offer repeated flushes if you miss the first chance. Yet I don't kill many. When one of these little fellows takes off, my gun automatically starts to mount—and just as automatically something within my psyche short-circuits my trigger response. Even when I shoot, it tends to be with the muzzle deliberately pointed somewhere alongside the target. I don't have this reaction with any other game bird. I can feel a sort of vengeful satisfaction when centering a long tailed, loud-mouthed cockbird, though I know he's never done anything to deserve such an attitude. I can take quiet pride in producing the mechanical know-how to center a passing dove at 45 yards, and a clean kill on a grouse keeps me somewhere on a cloud for days. Yet killing a woodcock always leaves me a little sad. Maybe it's because he strikes me as a comic creature, and there's so little in this world that makes me smile that I'm reluctant to destroy any part of it. Or maybe you're thinking this is all malarkey and I'm just trying to alibi my way out of the last few misses, huh? I've considered that possibility and discarded it. Not because I think I'm the world's greatest upland shot, but simply because I'm writing the truth as well as I can. I know what I do and how I do it. I'm just not sure why. Maybe it's better not to know. I said at the beginning of this chapter that the woodcock is a crazy bird. Maybe some woodcock hunters are too.

CHAPTER 3
Cottontail Rabbits

THERE WAS A CRISP SCUTTLING in the frosty November leaves that blanketed the woodlot. Then a flash of movement crossing in front of me, from right to left and angling slightly away through the gloomy woods. Suddenly, I recognized the racing creature for what it was—a cottontail rabbit. Not that I was unfamiliar with the species—Dad had brought them home from hunting trips as long as I could remember, and I'd seen many of them in the wild myself—but this one was

The late season, with snow on the ground, can provide some of the best action of the year, if you can face the frigid winds.

different. It was the first one I'd ever seen scrambling away through the woods when I had a gun in my hand and a hunting license on my back.

Somehow—I'll never be sure how it happened—the little Remington 20-gauge was at my shoulder and I swung and shot. The rabbit cartwheeled to a stop and lay there in the dead oak leaves, white belly shining, an instant kill. I just stood looking for a moment, then raced over to pick it up.

"Did you get him?" Dad shouted from somewhere off to my right.

"Sure," I answered, and I heard him and my uncle, Merle Stetler, roar with laughter. When I thought about it later, as I've done often through the years, I guess it did sound like a cock-sure kid's reply, but in all truthfulness I must say that the possibility I'd miss that shot never occurred to me. At the time I just stood there, holding the warm, dead, quivering bunny, overwhelmed with the knowledge that at last I was a genuine hunter. I'd been shooting since I was 4 years old—Daisy air rifles, a Crosman 22-caliber pellet gun, a 22 Winchester rifle and occasionally a shotgun of Dad's—and had probably killed thousands of sparrows, starlings and such stuff, but this rabbit was my first honest-to-gosh upland game. I was 12 years old.

My beginning as a hunter was probably typical. Practically every American kid's first game is a cottontail. That's as it should be, for the cottontail is this continent's All-American game animal. One subspecies or another is found over most of these United States, from sea level to well up in the Rocky Mountains, ocean to ocean and border to border, out in the boonies or in suburban gardens and backyards. He's available, he's hunted, and he's a great quarry that supplies an awful lot of sport to millions of outdoor people.

The cottontail's name comes from the nearly round, powder-puff tail. It's white underneath, primarily brown on top, to match the general coloration of the rest of him. When running away, the tail's white bottom is the most conspicuous part of the rapidly disappearing critter, so the name is logical. Common names usually are, even if they're not as precise as scientific monickers. *Sylvilagus floridanus* is what wildlife biologists call the basic species, in case you're interested.

The cottontail reaches a length of about 18 inches and a weight of 2 to 3 pounds, which makes it a sort of medium-size mammal. The hind legs are long and powerful, making long jumps and fast running easy. Ears are about 3 inches in length and highly flexible; they work like radar screens to detect even small noises nearby and, combined with the large eyes which are set high on the sides of the head to give perhaps 270-degree vision, make it difficult to get close to this animal without alarming it.

One key to finding a place to hunt is sharing your game with the landowner. It's amazing what a little common courtesy will do for hunter/farmer relations.

If we had to pick a couple of words to describe the cottontail, our first choices would be "ubiquitous" and "prolific." It's the second one that makes the first possible. This little critter is found almost everywhere for two basic reasons: It eats almost anything that grows; and it has a tremendous reproductive rate. Females often begin breeding at 6 months of age and three or four litters per year are not uncommon in warmer regions. After a gestation period of 28 to 30 days, the young are born, usually about four to eight. They weigh less than an ounce at birth and are helpless—near-naked, deaf and blind.

The female digs a nest before her youngsters are born. It's usually about the width of her body when she's lying down, 6 or 8 inches long, and 4 or 5 inches deep. It is rarely in thick cover but, due to her survival instinct, not far from some kind of escape route. The female lines the nest with dry grass or leaves or something similar, with a final layer of fur pulled from her own body. It would be hard to imagine a softer, warmer nest. A rougher cover that closely matches the surroundings then is added to conceal the nest from predators. That is not always successful, of course. Almost any creature that eats meat eats rabbit. Cats, dogs, weasels, crows, snakes, whatever—all eat rabbits, at least baby rabbits. In addition, unseasonably cold weather, floods, long wet spells or random fires kill many young cottontails. For one reason or another, it's likely that not more than half of the rabbits born survive long enough to leave the nest. Still, the species survives. It's been around since the late Eocene period, 60 million years, essentially unchanged, which is considerably longer than old Homo sapiens, so there's little point in our feeling too sorry for it. Chances are it'll still be here, hoppin' and boppin', long after we've vanished from the scene.

The female returns to the nest at dusk and dawn to feed her babies. She removes the concealing grasses and simply "rests" over the depression while the youngsters suckle. In only 2 weeks or so, the young rabbits leave their nest forever. In the meantime, the female has probably been impregnated again and is getting ready to raise another litter. That, plus the fact that female cottontails born in the early spring are often breeding themselves by late summer, helps account for the generally high population of rabbits in many parts of the United States. Even though few individuals, percentagewise, live for more than a year in the wild, many of these more than reproduce themselves during their brief lifespans.

Rabbits are not as numerous now, at least in the areas I'm familiar with, as they were when I was a kid. It's not that the rabbits aren't doing their part, but basically because the habitat that they like and require does not exist in the amount that it once did. New highways, shopping centers, suburban developments, private homes built in the country, jetports, industrial complexes, etc., remove countless acres from wildlife habitat each year. Many of us want these things—even demand them—but then gripe because we don't have the game to hunt that we used to have.

Furthermore, the thick fencerows, brushy hollows and swales, cedar swamps and overgrown sidehills that were common on farms in pre-World War II days have largely been eliminated by landowners whose primary interest is getting the maximum return possible from their land. This is understandable in an economic sense. Farming is a business just like any other, and when something is inefficient from a dollars-and-cents standpoint, that situation is going to be changed if at all possible. As a result, those "waste areas" have largely been eliminated and the space turned into crop-producing acreages. But from the hunter's viewpoint there's something sad about this. The chances are good many land-

Nick Sisley is a graduate of Carnegie Tech, a school which emphasizes the precision of mathematics. So what could be more logical than two barrels, two dogs, two rabbits? (He didn't say whether two shells did the job, but we'll give him the benefit of the doubt!)

owners feel the same way, at least from one angle, for most of this group feels a real kinship with the land and its animal populations. This is almost inevitable for anyone who grows up in a rural setting, as they have a direct year-round involvement with nature that urban dwellers simply don't experience. In fact, the farmer probably has a fuller understanding of the lives of all wild creatures in his area than hunters do, for most hunters come into contact with game only during the open season, while the farmer watches its activities—in a sense lives with it—through every month of the year. But no matter what interest in or fondness for a rabbit or quail or pheasant he feels, if his own economic situation requires that he eliminate the habitat necessary for a wild creature's survival, he's going to do it. And though we might loudly condemn him for this, the truth is, if we were in his shoes we'd do it too. It's easy to argue otherwise, from the comfort of our city or suburban homes, but that's how life is. We all ignore the other guy's problems. We expect him to disadvantage himself for our convenience and gripe because he doesn't do it. The fact of the matter is, countless farmers have for many years been putting up with all sorts of problems caused by unthinking hunters, and some of them are getting fed up with it. So they post their land against trespassing and they grow corn and oats and wheat where nature used to produce cottontails.

None of this is meant to suggest that rabbits are nonexistent, or endangered, or rare now. Even if they're not as plentiful as they were 40 years ago, quite a few can still be found. In a state like Missouri, which long has been something close to rabbit heaven, millions of cottontails are bagged by hunters each year, and even in a highly populated state like Pennsylvania over a million rabbits are normally taken during the 1-month open season. One of the problems with this, insofar as hunter satisfaction goes, is that Pennsylvania currently has over 1¼ million licensed resident hunters, which means that the season's average kill is less than one cottontail per hunter. That's hard for an older hunter to face up to. He can recall how it was when he was a kid—those seasons when, in his memory at least, he got his limit every time he went out. What few of them will admit is that not only was habitat much better back then, but also we had perhaps only one-third as many hunters. What this all boils down to is that there are still a lot of rabbits, even if fewer than during the legendary good ol' days, and it's still great fun to hunt them. In fact, the value we subconsciously assign to every quarry should go up for rabbits simply because they are not as common now. It certainly should obliterate remarks that were fairly common 30 or 40 years ago, such as one in a truly great book on grouse hunting. The author, recalling his younger days, remarked when they were toting up the day's bag: "We didn't count rabbits."

The comment was doubtless accurate reporting and, being the only unkind statement in the book, is forgivable. But I have to say that where I grew up we counted rabbits, and I still do. Not necessarily literal counting—whether I get one or four in a day, or none, doesn't matter greatly—but as something of value. They're not merely incidental targets sometimes taken while hunting other species, but highly admirable game animals in their own right.

Dogs and Rabbits

Some of my happiest hunting days have been those spent chousing out cottontails. The memories are not only of Dad and the rabbits and the guns and the beginnings of my hunting days, but also of the dogs. Sure, you can hunt rabbits without dogs—most of us have done it many times during our lives—but you just can't hunt them as well. Some things go together so perfectly that when one of the elements is missing the whole thing seems out of kilter. One of these combinations is cottontails and beagles. Alongside of this pair, ham and eggs or apple pie and ice cream are not even also-rans.

My dad grew up on a farm and dogs were simply part of such an existence then. But before I was born he was living and working in Danville, a small town along the Susquehanna River, 12 miles above the juncture of the North and West Branches. A bunch of dogs was impractical, but one wasn't, and there always seemed to be one around. Usually they were beagles—or "mostly" beagles—because rabbits were the critters primarily hunted by almost all the men and boys in town. Pheasants were coming along in those days and a few would be bagged each season, but all of the older hunters had grown up shooting cottontails, and they were the number one item on the agenda whenever anyone headed up along the river or toward one of the hollows that divided the river hills. So most everyone had a hound of some sort.

Rick was the first dog I really remember. We named him for Ricky Newman, the guy we got him from. He was on the big side for a beagle and when he walked he swung his rear end like Mae West, and in later years I came to realize that he never had been what anyone would call a great rabbit dog, maybe not even a good one. But he was my dog from the time I was in fourth grade until I went into the Army, which means I spent about half of my life to age 17 with him, and during those years I thought he was the greatest, the answer to any rabbit-finding problem as well as boon companion in any number of escapades, most of them unknown to my parents. Come to think of it, he was also the hero, or at least main character, in the first story I ever wrote for anyone but myself.

Even if he wasn't the world's greatest rabbit rouster or trailer, Rick did well enough. Dad and I normally had our share of bunnies at the end of the day, most of them rooted out by this slow old beagle that stuck his nose into every brushpile and corn shock and under every creekbank. Sooner or later he'd find what he was looking for, then there'd be a big hollow baying sound, like something coming out of a well, and a flurry of activity that quickly diminished to a more reasonable pace as Rick realized he couldn't catch that critter nohow and relaxed into a gait that convinced the rabbit his circle didn't really have to be ¼-mile in diameter. Before long the bunny would come hopping back—they almost always swing back to the area where first booted out—not taking Rick seriously at all. That was a mistake, of course, with Dad's L.C. Smith double 16 and my Ithaca Featherlight waiting somewhere in ambush.

One of the shots I remember best took place on a steep sidehill patched with sumac and brambles and laced with cattle trails. Neither Dad nor I had seen the rabbit until it suddenly appeared on one of the narrow bare trails between us, running flat out toward me with Rick right on its tail. Normally the dog would not have been that close; he apparently had stuck his nose right into the bunny's squat and both came boiling out of the thick stuff together. Neither Dad nor I could shoot without hitting the other, and I stood there, half crouched, gun at port arms, like the last tackler between a speeding ball carrier and the goal. Dad was yelling that I shouldn't shoot the dog—apparently unworried about the possibility I might shoot him. I was concentrating so hard that his shouts barely registered and the pair of racing critters hardly seemed to be moving though both had their accelerators to the floor. Only two or three steps from me, the rabbit suddenly realized something threatening was in its path and without slackening its pace in the slightest made a 90-degree turn to its right, heading full speed into a narrow opening that slanted down through the brush. Even as Rick was duplicating the maneuver, I snapped the Ithaca around and fired and the rabbit cartwheeled end over end, its nose

Open-country shots at rabbits are possible, they're just not probable. That's why short-barreled, open-choked guns are best for bunnies.

The brushy overgrowth of the spoil bank country of west-central Pennsylvania provides good rabbit hunting for those tough enough to hack it — if they're fast on the trigger.

taken off as if I had shot it sitting, and before it came to a stop Rick had grabbed it, probably not even knowing it was dead. I've never in my life made a shot where game, dog and gun were more intimately involved, and I've always been glad that Rick was the dog. Perhaps I was unfair to him earlier when I suggested he wasn't an outstanding rabbit dog. Maybe it was just his day-to-day style that wasn't overly impressive. When it came to getting the job done, he did all right. If you're a hunter, that's the important thing.

There should be some kind of dog in every kid's life. A beagle is a good choice. It's friendly, companionable, eager for most anything a youngster cares to try, and is also a working breed if anyone in the family hunts. Some of them, and Rick was one, even act as watchdogs, adopting a protective attitude toward family members. This might seem a bit difficult to believe, but I vividly recall the time when a man made a threatening movement toward my mother and suddenly found himself fighting off a king-size beagle which was doing his damndest to open up the guy's throat. The image still sends shivers along my spine. Anyway, I'm sure you understand why I remember Rick with fondness, though he's been gone for more than 30 years.

There were other beagles, mostly called Jack 'cause that's an easy name to holler, and one basset hound that didn't amount to much yet still was fun to be around. And that's why so many hunters like going for rabbits with dogs. It can be a glorious fall day, or it can be raining or snowing or sleeting or hailing, yet with a baying beagle on a hot trail, there's a sense of camaraderie that wipes out all the inconveniences and lets you remember only the good times.

Some dogs are highly useful on rabbits not because they run them as beagles or bassets do, but because they are good jumpers. They have no nose for trailing, though they often chase a rabbit as far as they can see it, but they are tremendous at finding bunnies and bouncing them out of the thick

stuff. This kind of dog, which often is a mongrel that makes itself useful around a farm, is usually a self-taught hunter that noses into every bit of cover—overgrown fencerows, junk-cluttered ravines, weedy creekbanks, cornfield edges, briar tangles—and rousts out any rabbit that's in there. If used in conjunction with a good trailer, the combination can be deadly. But if this is the only dog at hand, the gunner has to stay close and shoot fast, or wait till another cottontail is found, for once a rabbit is out of sight this kind of dog loses interest in it.

There are two things that make the beagle/bunny combination so appealing. First is the rabbit's built-in habit of circling. Cottontails have a fairly small home area and they don't particularly like to leave it. So when routed out of cover, one is likely to take off like a miniature thunderbolt, leaving the dog far behind, then slow down or even stop until it feels threatened again, when it once more easily outdistances the dog. But somewhere out yonder, usually not more than a couple of hundred yards at most and often less than that if cover is thick, the rabbit starts bending around, his mind apparently set on returning to the area where originally

Bob Mills and John Coleman share the spotlight with Don Lewis' longtime rabbit rouster, Rip. It was a pretty good day.

bounced out. Almost all rabbit hunters are born knowing this, the slow learner picking it up at his father's canvas-clad knee while the latest pup licks the peanut butter and jelly off his face. The hunters mentally follow the chase by listening to the tonguing of the dog, and that's the second big attraction of this kind of hunting. A beagle—or preferably two or three—chasing a bunny on a frosty November morning makes the kind of music the angels will play for me if I ever make it to the Happy Hunting Grounds.

There's a difference in the voices. Not only of different dogs, but from the same dog at different times. The occasional whine or near-whimper when he's eagerly searching out a hot scent but hasn't yet moved the rabbit. Sometimes a restrained yelp. Then the frantic *yip-yip-yip* when the rabbit explodes from its squat, followed by the rough barking of the early chase, then the steady quieter baying as both animals settle down for the longer trail. Sometimes way off in the distance it grows quiet, and the hunter waits and wonders what happened. Has the rabbit holed up or somehow fooled the dog—maybe doubled back unexpectedly, or made a long sideways leap and bent around in a different direction? Or has the dog simply lost the trail? But before long there's usually another flurry of sound and the gunner grins and tells himself that Ol' Rip never loses a trail like that . . . well, hardly ever . . . and when the music starts coming back his way he climbs up on a broad oak stump so he can watch both sides of the little ravine and lifts his gun to the ready position. And chances are pretty good that he'll soon get a glimpse of motion against the oak leaves up through the trees, maybe fast, maybe hopping, depending on how far back the dog is, and it'll be getting closer every second. When the time is right, the gun comes up and another good-eatin' cottontail goes into the gamebag. Usually. Sometimes the music is so good that he doesn't want it to stop, and he stands there on that old oak stump, gun cradled across his arms, just absorbing within himself the magical sounds and the ever-changing picture of the fall woods as the late afternoon light grows dim, until finally it's too dark to glimpse the rabbit or dog even when they pass by closely, two separate units bound into one entity by the now-mournful sound that drifts through the dark still woods. Finally, he calls the dog—it usually takes more than one call, sometimes a face-down hike through the thick pines to bring

R.M. Bell, the man who made a hunter out of the author, and Sport with a couple of cottontails taken in east-central Pennsylvania's Frosty Valley in the late '40s. Both Dad and Sport now do their hunting where the trails are always hot and the rain is always gentle and the little 16-gauge L.C. Smith double is the one gun in the rack that I'd never part with.

25

him in, but the man always gets him—and they make their way back to the pickup together, another memory tucked away for the time when the hills will be too steep, the snow too cold.

Go Slow and Get Game

It's not impossible to hunt rabbits without a dog, of course. In a pure sense, the best hunters probably do everything on their own. I had several uncles who were rabbit specialists, and though they had an assortment of dogs through the years, whenever I look back to the times I hunted with them, my memories are of their personal efficiency at finding and shooting rabbits. The best was George Buckley, a quiet, good-hearted man with a boyish smile who grew up when cottontails were numerous in this area. He was one of a large family and all the boys hunted.

It was always interesting to watch George. What I remember best was his casualness—even slowness. There's a tendency to equate quick smooth movements and fast gun handling with efficiency—the gunfighter syndrome, I suppose. Well, it's not really necessary to be fast on the draw to defend yourself against a cottontail. They hardly ever attack. Maybe George didn't feel any need for rushing or quick kills or whatever because hunting was a natural thing with him. He grew up doing it, learning from his father (my grandfather), Jack Buckley, a County Cork Irishman who came to this country as a teenager long before the turn of the century. The backyard of their home ran down to the Susquehanna, and in those days going hunting simply meant reaching behind the kitchen door for the old doubles and ambling down to the riverbank. If they had the time and the inclination, they might pole a rowboat across and kick through the hollows on the other side, mostly upriver from Blue Hill, and occasionally they made somewhat longer treks to farms which lay outside of town. But their hunting was mostly a nearby thing, probably more important for the food it supplied the big family than for recreation. When I hunted with George, though, it wasn't unusual for him to quietly say something that showed he appreciated the outdoors for more than its pantry aspects. This was in the late '30s and early '40s, long after my grandfather, whom I never knew, had died.

In the beginning, I had a tendency to rush, believing the more cover you hit the more game you'd see. It bothered me to wait for George, who just sort of poked along, rarely kicking the brush at all but looking, always looking, his gaze examining every bit of cover within a few yards of his feet. And he didn't carry his gun as I was certain any efficient hunter ought to, in both hands, muzzle up, ready to be thrown to the shoulder in a split instant to send a deadly shot charge on its way. Most of the time he carried it draped over his left elbow (he was a southpaw), muzzle pointing at the ground a few feet ahead of his knee-high rubber boots, a carry from which it obviously would take half a minute to get into action. It made me feel disloyal to think it, but George didn't really match my mental image of a hunter.

All of which shows how young and ignorant I was. While I was busting around, constantly trying to hit just one more patch of cover—the one that hopefully would hold a big woods bunny—George was looking into every tiny place that could conceal a rabbit *and seeing whatever there was to see.* It's strange that so many people believe they are hunting when in reality they are just wandering through the woods, gazing vaguely around themselves but never actually seeing the details of what is there. Sure, it's possible to stumble onto game that way, scare it out accidentally and kill it, but it's all sort of a random thing for which little credit can be taken. In contrast to this, George was *hunting.* He deliberately examined every bit of cover, looking into the brush and brambles, at the tiny oak-leaf-filled depressions between the roots of trees, under overhanging creekbanks, between the limbs of downed trees, under brushpiles. And after awhile it dawned on me that he was seeing more rabbits with his slow motion approach than I was with my constant hurrying. He'd often point one out to me. "There's his eye," he'd say. "See it shining against the leaves?" Eventually, the bright little spot would register on my gaze and then, magically, the whole

The end of a chase. The beagle doubtless has mixed feelings about this. The fun's over for him, at least for the moment, but chances are good he'll roust another cottontail out of its squat soon, and it'll all start over again.

Brushpile kickin' is an old, respected method of finding cottontails. Every kid with a gun has done it, sometimes successfully.

rabbit's body might appear and I'd stand and wonder why I couldn't see one like that myself.

I rarely did, even after I learned what to look for. Probably because pheasants were coming into their own at that time, my instinct was always to keep watching farther out, so if a bird flushed near the limit of my gun's effective range, I'd have a chance to drop him. I repeatedly told myself that this method gave me the best of both worlds, that I was ready for a rooster and at the same time would hear any rabbit I kicked out as it skittered away through the leaves. Often, this would prove true, yet I'm sure there were many times when my path didn't take me close enough to a bunny's squat to boot him out, so I never saw him at all. George, of course, saw most of them. He looked everywhere. When he finished with a creek-bottom or gully, there was no sense in anyone else going through it.

It wasn't only the thick covers that he understood. I well recall one afternoon when we were crossing a cut hayfield that didn't seem capable of concealing a mouse. It was a sunny day, but there was a chilly November wind, the kind that rabbits don't like because their soft fur has no guard hairs to turn its edge. I couldn't imagine one being in a place like this at such a time, but George pointed out a shallow dip ahead of us on the gentle sidehill. "That's the kind of place where a rabbit will squat in the sun," he said. "It's not deep but it's enough to protect him from the wind." He was right, too. One was there, and George kicked it out and killed it with an easy sweep of his old double after it got out 35 yards or so. I remember thinking I could have rolled it at least three times before he shot, but when he finally did fire the rabbit was out far enough that his tight choke didn't mangle it in the slightest. That was another lesson learned. As I suggested earlier, hunters of his generation shot mostly for the pot, not just for the score.

In line with that, it wasn't at all unusual for George or my dad or anyone else at that time to shoot a rabbit sitting. There's a tendency nowadays to feel that's unsporting, that

the animal has no chance at all when it doesn't realize it's seen and in mortal danger. In general, that's my own feeling. However, I'm of a later generation than they were and hunting to me is more a sport than a meal, so our basic objectives are somewhat different. A rabbit taken sitting was a good one for eating as you didn't have to worry about cracking a tooth on a chilled 6 pellet—a serious mishap back then. There wasn't much chance it was going to get away, either, which sometimes happens when you boot them out. On a few occasions, I have seen sitting rabbits missed when the hunter tried to just nip the end of the nose and missed altogether. Quite often, these were killed on the follow-up running shot, though. Fact is, a damn small percentage of the shots I saw Dad and George and their brothers try were misses. They grew up when money was scarce and shells were valuable, so when a gun went boom something usually died.

Dad made the longest shot I ever saw on a cottontail. I was working the edge of a field and he was below me on a steep wooded sidehill. It was late afternoon, getting dark in the woods, when I heard his L.C. Smith go off and he hollered, "Look at this shot." He walked and walked and walked, until I was beginning to think it was some sort of joke. Then he bent down and picked up a rabbit. "Seventy-six long steps," he yelled. "With the open barrel and 7½ shot." If anyone is critical of an occasional sitting rabbit taken with that gun, this one shot should square things up.

Interestingly, the longest shot I ever made with a smoothbore was with the same gun, years later. We were then living on the outskirts of town in a home Dad had built while I was in the Army during World War II. A large field lay behind the house, with a small tree-bordered creek along the far edge. From our back porch to a large willow was exactly 85 yards. I had a rifle target set up against the bank and had stepped it off many times. One day I happened to look out the window of our den and saw a crow feeding in the field, probably 65 yards away. The gun cabinet stood nearby and I reached in, got Dad's 16-gauge and a pair of shells that were handy, a high-

Most youngsters do their first upland hunting in rabbit cover — and these are the hunts they'll remember all their lives. (Photo by Joe Osman.)

brass load of 6s and a low-brass 7½. I put the 6s in the modified tube, the light load in the improved cylinder barrel and eased the muzzle out of the window. I didn't think I had any chance, so decided to try the crow on the ground, using the tight barrel and heavy load. I saw the pattern hit in the dust all around the crow, but apparently not a single pellet touched him 'cause he took off frantically, low to the ground, crossing from right to left. I swung somewhere ahead of him and hit the front trigger. *Pow!* That poor old crow was dead in the air. It just collapsed in a black ball and splashed into a small pool in the creek a couple of yards beyond my rifle target. But those couple of yards meant it was at least 87 yards from the gun, and that's a right fer piece to kill anything with a field load of 7½s out of an improved cylinder bore. Anyone who thinks otherwise is welcome to try. The kill, of course, was largely

luck, but it's still a shot I like to recall at odd moments.

Both of these shots were somewhat unusual because of the ranges at which they gave instant kills. I don't recall examining either Dad's rabbit or the crow to see where they were hit, but chances are good that a pellet got into the brain of each. That's the only placement that usually gives such quick results. It doesn't take a lot of energy to kill a rabbit, but you can't expect a single pellet through the body to be effective. It may be deadly in the sense that the little animal is going to die, but chances are it will be at least a couple of hundred yards away, which means that it probably will not be recovered by the hunter unless he has a good dog. On several occasions I've found dead rabbits which were still warm, indicating they had been shot only a short time previously, and in these instances each had a single pellet through the body. No hunter

Don Lewis looks too neat here, his SKB too new, to have taken this bunch of rabbits by himself. Helen probably shot 'em and then took the picture. She spoils him something awful for some reason.

tries for such results, of course, but they happen and they point up the necessity of following up every shot on game, if at all possible.

A good hound can more than earn his keep in the thick cover where cottontails are often shot. When the hunter has only a glimpse of a white tail before the rabbit vanishes, and gets off a shot in a fraction of a second, it's sometimes impossible to know if he hit or not. The dog makes the difference. Some hounds will retrieve rabbits. So will some bird dogs, and personally I think they should be encouraged in this if the owner shoots rabbits. Usually the hounds that don't retrieve will stay with the dead animal, worrying it a bit until you get there, and for all practical purposes that's as good as a retrieve. Even without a dog, the hunter can sometimes find a rabbit he's shot at, just by following along in the general direction it was going when last seen. A lot of times a wounded rabbit will go only a short distance before dying, and will be found stretched out in a running posture right out in the

In winter, rabbit shooting can require a lot of cold hiking across wide windy stretches, the shots few and far between — and long when they are presented. But it's still a good time to be afield, as any hunter knows.

open. If on its side, the white belly hair is easily visible against the usual dead leaf litter. You can't count on that, but you should always make the search.

Shot Size and Chokes

Medium size shot makes the best choice for rabbit shooting, from 8s at the small end to 5s at the big, with 6s probably the best single choice. Best choke depends on the average cover hunted, with a Skeet gun or IC boring tops for working the choppings and briar patches cottontails like. However, some states have late seasons on rabbits, often after Christmas and into the real winter weather. Most cover is gone at this time, tramped down by earlier bird hunters or destroyed by frost, snow and wind, and this improves visibility. Modified or even full choke barrels can be useful at this time of year, for rabbits are often visible at long distances against the snow. The last rabbit hunt I made was under these conditions. Chuck Fergus, Fred Hartman and I moved 13 cottontails during a half-day hunt, which is good for our area in winter, and a reasonably tight choke—say modified—was about perfect for all the shooting we got.

If you are in tight cover most of the time, it's impossible to get a barrel that's too open. Where you're shooting only 10 yards or so, which occurs more often than might seem possible to hunters with little experience on cottontails, even an improved cylinder choke makes a mighty small pattern that can destroy a small game animal that's centered. I got a graphic illustration of this some years back. I was working around a very steep sidehill near the remains of an old quarry when a rabbit erupted from almost under my boots. In a moment it was going to vanish over a slight bulge in the terrain, so I knew I had to shoot immediately or have no

chance at all. I swung the Browning Sweet 16 hard and hit the trigger automatically, and under normal circumstances I think I'd have centered that disappearing bunny. But I doubt that a single pellet ever reached him. In one of those freakish shots that happen now and again, I'd slapped the trigger just as my gun's muzzle lined up with a small hickory tree a few feet ahead. It was maybe 3 inches in diameter, and my load of 7½s cut it off completely—just sort of took a chunk out of it some 3 feet from the ground. The top section dropped vertically alongside the bottom part and stood there for a few seconds as if undecided what to do. Then it slowly fell over, tilting away from me. I was so surprised by what my shot had done, and so fascinated with watching the results, that I lost all track of the rabbit. For all I know, it's going yet. I sure never touched a hair on it. Anyway, this example shows the power and concentration of even small shot out of an improved cylinder choke when the range is short.

One of the best rabbit outfits I ever saw belonged to a farm kid. It was an old double that had lost the front 6 inches or so of both barrels, probably as a result of being fired when the muzzles were plugged with mud after a fall. After things were squared up with a hacksaw, the tubes were maybe 22 inches long, which meant they were true cylinder bore. The experts claim that a couple of thousandths of choke will give better patterns than true cylinder, sort of evening things up on the way out. They're probably right, and a good gunsmith can get these results with a jug choke. But this kid was completely unaware of such niceties and wouldn't have spent the money had he known about 'em. I wouldn't blame him for ignoring them, either. No one and no gun could improve on the way he killed rabbits in the winter swamps he haunted, taking shots at any range he could see them—like from 6 feet to 12 yards. There'd be a flash of brown against the cattails, activated by either him or his little three-color mongrel, then a blur of movement as the gun came up and *Boom!* Dead bunny. He was so efficient it was scary. He had a reaction time like an electric trigger, just an automatic non-thinking response to a stimulus. What a partner he'd have been when it was housecleaning time in northern Germany in the spring of '45.

I've always been partial to double guns for upland hunting, but I've got to admit that my most efficient outfit for rabbit shooting is the Browning Sweet 16. Mine has to be one of the ugliest guns in creation, what with a stock that's been shortened drastically and a barrel that's scarcely 22 inches overall, including the Poly-Choke. But when it comes to killing, this is my personal Number One. It fits me perfectly and it's just plumb poison on game. There have been several seasons when I killed everything I shot at with it, and even when I'm having a bad day it sometimes comes through. For instance, I recall a particularly impressive bit of missing on one cottontail. We were actually hunting pheasants, but my daughter would rather eat rabbit, so unlike several friends I never pass them up. Anyway, in a brambly wooded corner between two weedfields a rabbit suddenly squirted out, dodging and twisting through the thick stuff as I proceeded to shoot, and shoot, and shoot a third time, each load of 7½s going precisely where it had been only a fractured second before. As I tripped off the shot that emptied my gun, the rabbit abandoned the noisy premises and raced down a sort of path along a narrow fencerow that divided the two fields. I grabbed another shell out of my vest and threw it into the open loading port of the Browning, just as the rabbit made a right-angle turn into the fencerow. As it went out of sight, I hit the bolt release button to chamber the shell, and a moment later the rabbit appeared in the other field, running broadside, and I rolled it. Ever since, I've had second thoughts about the ethics of that shot—when you miss a critter three times in a couple of seconds, do you really deserve another shot?—but at the time I was all caught up in the action and not really thinking about anything except connecting. At any rate, the episode does show how this little Browning comes through sometimes despite the ineptitude of the guy shooting it. It also shows how a guy who has been hunting cottontails for almost four decades can still get excited when one goes out. And that's another thing I like about 'em. They make me realize I still get a kick out of hunting.

Rifles, Handguns and Rabbits

There are times and places when rifles or handguns serve well for rabbits, too. I'm sure we could dream up a situation where we might make an argument for most any caliber, but as a normal thing only a rimfire .22 would be used on rabbits. Again, there are places where an autoloading rifle would provide a lot of sport as you tried to connect with a fast moving cottontail, but in many areas the safety problem would argue against such a gun. It takes a lot of lonesome acreage to permit the kind of shooting such an outfit brings to mind. When you have a cartridge that can be dangerous at more than a mile, it just isn't sensible to let yourself get carried away with a fast-firer in your hands. What this means is that a rabbit hunter should use a rifle only under conditions which he himself can closely control. His psychological attitude should be that of the sniper rather than the submachine gunner: He should be a calm, cool, thinking shooter rather than a fast-reacting, impulsive gunnerman.

Anyone who can honestly say that he qualifies in this respect can find rifles a real challenge for rabbits. He's not as likely to get a limit as the shotgunner, but he can have fun. Results are usually better in the winter season, when fewer hunters are around and game can be seen at longer range. A

After four consecutive wet days after rabbits in cover like this (note the hip boots), John Behel said to hell with it and became a turkey hunter.

warm sunny day after a cold snap can bring rabbits out to feed on south-facing slopes, and the guy with a carefully zeroed-in scoped .22 can have a lot of fun. Any modern .22 is accurate enough to shoot cottontails in the head at 50 yards; in fact, some of today's sporters will hit a nickel most every shot at that distance with target ammo, if the shooter does his part. Even Long Rifle hollow points will do almost this well, if you find a make your gun likes. This is in contrast to the results delivered by ammo of several decades back, when hollow points tended to group poorly at best. Most current stuff will shoot far better than the average rifleman can hold under field conditions. For cottontails, hollow points are not necessary, though, as conventional bullets have plenty of killing power and destroy less meat.

I like bolt actions, so use this type for all my rimfire rifle hunting, but I have friends who prefer lever and pump guns and they do as well or better than I. We all use scopes, and prefer the big game designs built on 1-inch tubes rather than the so-called .22 scopes which have smaller fields, less light transmission and more critical eye relief. Nevertheless, good shooting can be done with these less expensive models if they are properly mounted so that a full field is immediately visible when the gun is shouldered. A magnification of 2½x is almost always enough, though on rare occasions—as when you're trying to sort a rabbit's head out of some shadowy brush maybe 60 yards away—4x might offer an advantage. I have one .22 that carries a 6x Leupold, and it's a super-accurate combination for winter shooting at long range. It's heavy and a specialized outfit that was really built for squirrel sniping, but when conditions are right, it's impressive.

I've mentioned a reluctance to shoot sitting rabbits with a shotgun. Though it makes for good eating, I don't like to do it. Quite a few years ago it struck me that the solution might be to use a handgun for squatters. I looked the field over and decided that the lightweight Ruger Single-Six was just the ticket for this chore. I got one and a Keith-designed Lawrence rig to carry it and took to the field, feeling something like Billy the Kid reincarnated. A bit surprisingly, the idea worked well. The little Ruger was easy to carry and very accurate. On these occasions when I missed in spite of the gun's efficiency and the rabbit departed forthwith, I could let it dangle (hammer down on a fired case) from the trigger guard while I got the shotgun into operation. The single action design made it safe to handle this way, something that wouldn't have been possible with an auto-loader and which would have been very questionable with a double action revolver. Eventually I quit carrying a handgun, but there's no reason to think it won't work if all the requirements are understood and met.

Field-Dressing and Cleaning

Cottontails are the easiest upland game to field-dress, I believe, even easier than doves. Immediately after shooting, I hold the rabbit belly up in one hand, pull the fur off from ribs to anus, squeeze the back to tighten the belly skin and slit open from end to end. Any knife will cut through rabbit ribs as easily as belly skin, so go all the way up to the throat. Then just flip everything out. You might have to pull some odds and ends loose, but there's nothing difficult about it. Some hunters feed the entrails to their dogs, claiming it makes them better hunters, but I've a hunch this is one of those old tales from the hills. Conversely, it's a scientific fact that rabbits are often hosts to tapeworms, and the dog that eats rabbit guts can well end up with this parasite himself. So don't let him eat these innards. I don't skin rabbits in the field as the fur keeps the meat clean while in the shooting coat. But I do finish the job as soon as I get home. The easiest way is to chop off the head and feet with a hatchet, cut crossways through the fur at the middle of the back and pull it both ways. It will peel right off, leaving a clean pink carcass that I soak in cold saltwater overnight. Shot-up areas can be cut out and discarded, but unless they're pretty bad you might be surprised how well the saltwater will take care of things. We usually cut it into five serving pieces—two hindquarters, two shoulder sections complete with front legs, and the back from which the ribs are removed.

A lot of upland hunters ignore cottontails, apparently feeling it's beneath them to shoot land-bound critters. That's silly snobbery, in my opinion, but I don't try to change their minds. The ones they pass up can supply me and some friends with many days of enjoyment.

Field-dressing rabbits is easy. You open 'em stem to stern with your knife, flip out everything, and stuff them in your game bag. Remove head, feet and hide when you get home. The fur protects the meat while rabbit is in your coat.

CHAPTER 4

Snowshoe Rabbits

IN THE NEIGHBORHOOD where I grew up, if a kid couldn't find something, he was likely to say, "It's like looking for a black cat in a coal mine at midnight." (Coal is that black hard stuff they take out of the ground and used to burn in furnaces before oil and gas got popular.) We lived not far from the greatest anthracite region on earth, so the analogy was reasonable. But if we had been even closer, in the Pocono Mountains, say, the expression might have been, "Like looking for a snowshoe rabbit in a cedar swamp in December." I like this one better, for several reasons. I like rabbits, any

kind, better than cats, and I sure prefer a frozen snow-covered swamp to a coal mine. With claustrophobia like I've got, there's no way I'm going down in one of those things. Anyway, snowshoe rabbits supply some excellent sport in northeastern Pennsylvania's hills, among other places, though for some reason not a lot gets written about them.

Snowshoes are much bigger than cottontails, almost twice as heavy at maximum weight. They have long ears, powerful hind legs that seem disproportionately huge even for this kind of critter, and big feet that grow long coarse hair on the soles

(Left) Dick Fuller of Emporium, Pennsylvania, and one of the four-legged ghosts. Snowshoes rarely come easy, so getting one makes a hunter feel that he's done something. They're bigger than cottontails, run well, don't hole up and are good eating. What more does a winter-hunter need? (Photo by Dave Drakula.)

(Below) This is why they call him "Bigfoot." These oversize hairy pads make it easy for a showshoe to "snowshoe."

When the snow is deep, it can take even long-legged dogs a while to bring a white rabbit around. So you wait. That can be a chilly business but it beats watching television on a Saturday afternoon. (Photo by Thad Bukowski.)

This one tried crossing an old woods road, was exposed for a second, and was intercepted by a load of 6s.

Sometimes snowshoe country can give you a lonesome feeling. But the Jeep has to be over there somewhere . . . doesn't it?

in winter to serve as snowshoes—thus their common name. During the warmer months, a snowshoe is generally gray-brown in color, somewhat darker down the middle of the back and toward the rump. As with the cottontail, the snowshoe's tail is dark on top and white below. In late fall, the snowshoe's pelt turns white, except for the tips of the ears which usually remain black. This change is nature's way of camouflaging the animal in snow country. However, temperature has nothing to do with the switch to white in winter or back to brown in spring. The controlling factor is light. As days get shorter in autumn, less light enters the snowshoe's eyes. This has an effect upon the pituitary gland, which during the fall molt shuts off the production of pigment for the new fur. It thus comes in white, to blend with the snows of winter. During the following spring, the increased light of the longer days reverses the process and the warm weather coat is brown. Because these changes have nothing to do with temperature or the color of the ground cover, in years of little snowfall the snowshoe rabbit's white color makes him extremely conspicuous in the woods.

Actually, the snowshoe is not a rabbit at all, but a hare. Because its fur changes color, it's called a varying hare. Both rabbits and hares are members of the same family, *Leporidae,* but they belong to different genera. The snowshoe is a member of the genus *Lepus,* while the cottontail is in genus *Sylvilagus.* Whereas cottontails are blind and nearly naked at birth, newborn hares are comparatively well developed. The males often fight for the right to breed receptive females, but ignore the young which result from their attentions. Females have one to three litters per summer, usually of two or three young, though as many as six might be born. Gestation period is 36 days. The young hares, called leverets, have fine grayish-brown fur, weigh 2½ to 3 ounces, and begin to nurse almost immediately. They start moving around as soon as they are dry, and after 10 days or so are nibbling green vegeta-

33

Typical snowshoe rabbit country. When snow fills the laurel like this, white rabbits are invisible. (Photo by Dave Drakula.)

dators, particularly the Canadian lynx. Snowshoes like room to move about, but when the population peaks in a favorable region it's not uncommon to have several of these big hares on an acre, which means there can be more than a thousand on a square mile. That's a lot of critters, and the number drops rapidly when nature's various controls take over, hits bottom in about 5 years and then starts to climb again. Maximum population densities like this are more common in southern Canada than in the U.S. In the "up" years, predators like the large hawks and the snowy owl eat well, but chances are diseases and parasites have more effect on the total number of snowshoes than the big predators.

Not only winged predators like snowshoes. People eat them, too. Sometimes more than they care to. Some years ago Wes Bower and I were moose hunting in upper Quebec, working out of a French-speaking outfitter's lodge. The accommodations were more than adequate, especially for guys like us who were used to bushwacking it with a tent and sleeping bags. But the main meal every evening was built around either snowshoe rabbit or spruce grouse snared by the ancient camp handyman who earned his keep by odd chores like this. He was a nice old guy who still pulled his weight, but I'll tell you—a feller can get tired of over-cooked snowshoe rabbit after a week or so, especially when there's no ketchup to help things along.

Besides providing food for anything in the region that eats meat, snowshoes provide the basic material for an indispensable piece of equipment in the Canadian bush, the sleeping robe. Many years ago, Col. Townsend Whelen, the great gunwriter, told about this in one of his books or articles, and the idea has fascinated me ever since. He described how the Indians cut snowshoe pelts into spirals about 2 inches wide, sewed them into long strips and weaved these into a sort of comforter. Because no rabbit fur is highly durable, this furry comforter was often sandwiched between two light wool blankets, making a rig that provided comfortable sleeping in extreme temperatures. I doubt that it would equal a high quality goosedown mummy bag for pure efficiency, but it's a prime example of the way woods-wise people utilize available material to wrest comfort out of a sometimes inhospitable environment.

Snowshoes aren't always seen in great numbers, even in the wilderness. One of the lonesomest, most forlorn looking critters I ever saw was a white rabbit, out in west-central Idaho, some years back. Several of us were elk hunting in the high country west of the Payette Lakes, and one day I drifted down off a ridge, through some boggy stuff and into one of the most depressing spots I've ever seen. It was like something out of the nether regions . . . black, foul, dead. The trees—conifers—were small by Idaho standards, 4 to 8 inches at ground level, and they were all a charcoal gray color, dead. There was almost no brush. The ground between them was dead, a sort of slippery claylike mud that was also black. The whole area smelled with a smell I didn't recognize. By the time I'd gone 100 yards, all I wanted was to get out of there. Idaho is like a second home to me, and that was the only piece of it I'd ever seen that repelled me. As I hurried along, a spot of white suddenly appeared up ahead. Inside all that blackness, it looked like something from another world. It was coming closer, and I automatically raised the .338 to look through the scope. It was a snowshoe, looking as lost and bewildered as I felt. For a moment the cross hairs rested on its shoulder, but nothing could have made me touch the trigger, and it soon disappeared from my sight. I don't know if it ever saw me. Even if it did, I doubt that it ever thought about me in any way. But I've thought about it many times through the years, and always hoped it found its way back to the green country. Not that it could have made much difference in the

tion. They are on their own at 5 or 6 weeks of age.

Snowshoes, in one or another of a dozen minor variations, are found from Alaska, south to our Pacific Northwest, down through the Rockies to Colorado and northern New Mexico, and from Saskatchewan east to the mountains of West Virginia and northeast to Rhode Island. Their favorite habitat is marshy woods, logged-off areas growing back to brush, particularly if parts are on the wet side, cedar, spruce and tamarack swamps, and thick stands of aspen, conifers and poplars, all of which provide food for this big-eared critter. They don't like areas which have recently been clearcut, but will filter into such places after brush regenerates.

Populations are cyclic, maximums being reached at about 10-year intervals, and are influenced by the presence of pre-

end. Where our tent was pitched that year, there's a ski lift now.

Most snowshoe hunting experiences aren't so depressing, thank God. Our usual procedure is to pile into the old Japanese Jeep and point it toward the wooded hills of northeastern Pennsylvania. (There's always a temptation to say mountains, but after a baker's dozen jaunts to Idaho, Wyoming, Colorado, northeastern New Mexico, and such, the hills of home, cold and desolate as they might be at certain times of the year, just don't seem to require that term. No matter. They're high and steep enough, when the snow is on them.) A lot of that country is flat-topped, though, or reasonably so, and somewhat strangely a significant percentage of it is swamp country. Not Okefenokee-type stuff, but cold swamps, at least at the time of year we're talking about. There are small lakes, bogs and marshy areas, tangles of cedars and alders and scrub oaks and rhododendron, country where, when the temperature and humidity are right, layers of fog and mist and even rain or snow clouds shroud everything like a ghost-blanket. But this seems a normal thing up there, expected during snowshoe season. And even the misty days sometimes are broken by moments of clear sunshine when the snow sparkles and glitters as if with an inner life of its own, and the barking of the hounds is sharp-edged and close-sounding, rather than forlorn as distant bells.

Again, you don't have to have dogs to hunt snowshoes, but two or three good ones add something special to the hunt. Bigger, long-legged hounds work better in the snow than small ones. This big hare runs well ahead of the dogs, and he doesn't have the cottontail's tendency to hole up when the pressure gets high. Maybe that's because there are no woodchuck dens in his typical home country. The snowshoe doesn't like to leave his own territory, either, so will circle back when pushed, though not always so precisely to his starting point as the cottontail. Or maybe it seems that way because the snowshoe brought back is not necessarily the one the dog started out with. When there are a lot of them in an area, it can be difficult for a dog to stay on an individual track. No matter. So far as the hunter is concerned, one of these four-legged ghosts is as good as another when it goes by him.

A snowshoe can be truly hard to see in the winter woods. Motionless, he's almost literally invisible, his black ear tips only aiding his camouflage as he squats in the shadowy whiteness. His black shiny eye, because it is round and thus unnatural, is the only real giveaway, and experienced hunters learn to look for this. Often tracks go all directions in a swamp, but a rabbit is never seen—and sometimes it seems you are watching a set of tracks appearing in the cold white stuff as if by magic, for the critter leaving them is but a vague fleeing image at best! That's one of the weirdest experiences in the woods, and it can make you clutch your shotgun for reassurance against the supernatural forces that sometimes seem to dwell in these winter swamps.

The thing to do, of course, when you do glimpse one of these white-on-white targets, is shoot. They're bigger than cottontails, but a load of 6s will handle most opportunities, particularly if you're using 1¼ ounces or more. For longer shots ahead of the dogs, 5s are fine, but in the thick cover where snowshoes are usually booted out, ranges tend to be short.

A lot of walking under difficult conditions can be expected, so a lightweight gun is convenient. A repeater has the extra shot which can be worth its weight in platinum to the guy who has slogged through deep snow for hours in hopes of putting out just one of these critters—and that's not unusual when populations are down—but a double offers the instantaneous choice of two chokes, which also can mean the difference between success and failure. So, take your choice.

Despite the fact that cold windy weather is normal when hunting snowshoes, don't overdress. A lot of exercise is involved, and you can work up a sweat in a hurry even when the temperature is close to zero. Gloves, insulated boots, wool socks and underwear, woolshirt and maybe a down vest, all beneath a windproof coverall, make a good combination. A down jacket in a stuff sack, toted in the game vest, makes it easy to stand motionless for a long stretch when waiting for the dogs to bring a white bunny back. So, try snowshoe hunting. It's a great way to cure the winter blahs.

The rabbit went through there so you can, too, right? Well, maybe. At least you can try. But keep the gun muzzle out of the snow.

CHAPTER 5

Mourning Dove

OFTEN, THEY'RE SEEN first as dots in the sky, just specks above the horizon perhaps a ¼-mile away. A neophyte hunter might not even recognize them, or if he does he might ignore them, thinking they are too far away to be of interest. What he doesn't realize as he glances away is that by the time he's taken six or eight breaths, those dots can be full-size mourning doves flashing over his stand at 50mph. From tiny points in the distance they suddenly metamorphose into gray streaks like pencil lines scribbled against the sky, and then, even more suddenly, they're gone. And it's not only the new shooter who gets caught flat-footed—or maybe gun-in-handed would be a more accurate term. Longtime dove shooters also get caught looking the wrong way, sometimes recovering just in time to see what it's now impossible to shoot at, other times completely left in the lurch, only the derisive shouts, or shots, of their buddies calling attention to their embarrassment.

Doves do you like that. Not always, of course. No other American game bird is taken in such numbers as *Zenaida macroura,* the mourning dove. Most current estimates put the annual national harvest at something over 50 million with a few wildlife biologists setting the total as high as 75 million. That's an awful lot of birds, but it's only 10-15 percent of the overall population, and since the annual mortality rate on this species, whether hunted or not, is about 70 percent, those taken by shooters have no significant impact. In fact, hunting is a plus factor, for the doves shot are taken home and eaten, thus serving a worthwhile purpose instead of going to waste when death is due to other factors.

The mourning dove has the perfect answer for its high mortality rate—baby doves. Doves nest from the southern Canadian provinces down through the U.S. and Mexico into Central America. A mated pair will build a ramshackle nest, usually fairly close to the ground, or even on the ground in areas where trees are scarce. They nest in suburban areas as willingly, it seems, as in farmlands. We've had them nesting in some small pines in our backyard for years. On rare occasions, particularly in the South, a pair of doves will produce half a dozen hatches in a season, usually of two nestlings each, and birds born in the spring sometimes have offspring of their own in the fall of the same year. Birds breeding in northern regions are not so prolific; two or three hatches per season is more reasonable here.

Chicks hatch after a 2-week incubation. They are barely an inch long at birth and differ from our other game birds in that they are altricial: They come into the world blind and practically naked. But they grow up in a hurry. Fed first on pigeon's milk, an extremely nourishing substance secreted from glands in the crop walls of both parents, then on seeds and other solid food, they quickly gain weight and feather out. Less than 2 weeks after hatching, they are making short flights, and soon they're on their own. This doesn't bother the parents in the slightest. Almost immediately, they're producing another pair of offspring. As a result, even though nestings fail for one reason or another, going into the fall hunting season there are upwards of 500 million mourners in the U.S. That's a bunch of game birds by any reckoning.

An adult mourning dove is a beautifully shaped bird, not

T.R. Them with a mourner he kicked out of a weedfield and dropped when he tired of waiting for some birds to pass. Jump shooting doesn't usually produce a lot of doves, but it breaks the monotony of waiting when things are slow.

High weeds can make an excellent hiding place, but doves that fall into such cover are difficult to find. It's best to drop them in open fields.

big—usually between 4 and 5 ounces—but super streamlined. It's about 12 inches long, from pointed beak to tip of pointed tail, with a wingspread of about the same measurement. Wings are pointed too, and swept back slightly. Even sitting motionless in a dead branch it looks like it's going 60 miles per hour, and given a bit of tailwind it might actually make that. Its topside feathers are gray to my eyes, though many hunters speak of brownish tints. When the sun hits one right, an iridescence about the neck feathers, particularly of adult males, can be seen on birds in the hand. Tail feathers are darker, with occasional white spots, breast feathers softer and paler, and there's a small black spot behind and below the eyes.

Because they're migratory birds, doves come under the basic jurisdiction of the U.S. Fish & Wildlife Service, which has divided the 48 contiguous states into three management units. The Eastern Unit is generally east of the Mississippi River, the Western Unit consists of the seven far western states, and the Central Unit lies between those two. Seasons and bag limits are set by the individual states within a framework laid down by the federal agency. Seasons are comparatively long—several months—and limits generous, usually 12 birds per day or thereabouts. At this writing, 32 states have open seasons on mourning doves, most of those which have no seasons being located in the upper half of the country and east of Idaho.

There are good numbers of doves in all the remaining states except Alaska, so hunters could benefit from open seasons in these regions. Political pressures from anti-hunters and persons who think of the dove as only a songbird apparently account for the lack of this hunting opportunity. This is unfortunate, not only from the standpoint of those who like to hunt but also because it shows a lack of understanding on the part of a large percentage of our voters—a lack which is probably our fault. The anti-hunters are simply that—against hunting

There's no reason not to be comfortable while waiting for doves. A folding seat under a tree and a cooler of Cokes in the Jeep make life easy in September.

no matter what—and we're not going to change their minds. But the vast majority of Americans are neither pro- nor anti-hunting. They're largely uninterested in this sport. If they do not understand that wildlife is a renewable resource, one that will not only survive but flourish as long as it has suitable habitat and its hunting is regulated by a governmental authority whose first concern is the welfare of the species, that means we hunters have not made them aware of the facts. So we've mostly ourselves to blame when hunting opportunities are taken away from us. At least one of the states which is now closed to dove hunting has been open in the past. That should be a lesson to us, for if one species can be taken off the open list, it's not impossible that others will be too. It's a shame that hunters so often wait until their sport is in extreme danger before uniting to do something about it. As much as most of us dislike the political involvement that such action requires, that's where things get decided in the end. As a start on an individual basis, each of us should take advantage of every opportunity to explain the basics of wildlife management, seasons and bag limits, etc., to any nonhunter who will listen. They're the ones who cast most of the votes, so it's up to us to explain the facts so they can understand the hunter's view-point.

Hunting and Habitat

Dove hunting is different than any other upland hunting. For the most part it might be viewed as waterfowl shooting on dry land. That's because doves are usually taken by pass shooting, much as a duck or goose hunter takes these bigger birds from his blind. In fact, most dove hunters shoot from brushy positions which might well qualify as blinds since they conceal the hunter or at least break up his outline, while others actually build blinds of a sort. For several reasons,

(Above) You can get a stiff neck watching for doves to come in—the dog, too. But if you relax for even a moment they'll be in and gone before you realize it.

(Left) Hayes Englert and his grandson with the boy's first dove. Though not very big, this bird is something the youngster will long remember.

38

they're usually not as elaborate as waterfowl blinds. First, because it isn't necessary, as doves aren't as wary as ducks, and second, because it's often necessary to shift shooting positions to cover incoming flight lanes, so a permanent gussied up design isn't very practical.

The first thing to do in a dove shoot is find the birds. You do this by looking for feeding areas. Doves eat seeds almost exclusively, the exact kinds varying with the part of the country they're in. In east-central Pennsylvania, where I do most of my shooting, weed seeds such as those of foxtails are a special favorite, along with waste corn, wheat, peas and sorghum. Sunflower seeds and peanuts are eaten when available, along with other grass seeds, fruit seeds, etc. Doves eat early in the day, go to water, mostly loaf during midday, usually congregating with a bunch of buddies to talk things over—what else is there for a feller to do on those long golden fall afternoons?—and when the sun starts to lower they go and eat some more.

Despite their melancholy mourning, doves are not loners. In fact, they're highly gregarious, often being seen sprinkled over a dead tree like Christmas tree ornaments, or perhaps lined up on utility wires as if assigned sitting space by a mathematician. When a single is seen, he's usually going somewhere fast, trying to find his friends.

They also feed in bunches, hundreds sometimes collecting in a newly picked Pennsylvania grainfield. That can be impressive as blazes to a shotgunner who has spent many long hours trying to boot just one grouse out of the grapevines, but it pales to insignificance alongside the thousands that occasionally assemble to feed in some fields of the Deep South. That's the kind of opportunity most of us never see, but the fact remains that even in "poor" dove country the shooting can be fantastic by most standards.

At any rate, you find doves by locating their feeding areas. Sometimes a friend will give you a lead to them (and any hunter who will do this is really a friend!), sometimes you get results by talking to farmers, watching for fields to be cut, etc.; but usually you find them by spending time in rural areas in late afternoon, watching for moving birds. Binoculars are helpful. With them, you can sit in a parked car and sometimes see birds moving against the sky a mile or more away. They might be going to feed or to roost, depending on the time of day, but sooner or later you'll get some flight lanes located. Then you find where they're feeding and you do whatever is necessary to get permission from the landowner to hunt. Often this is just a courteous request, along with a promise (carried out) not to cause any damage to his property, or to litter, or to shoot in an unsafe manner. Litter includes empty shotshells—especially plastics—and the discarded material from dressed doves. *Don't* clean them in the farmer's field. It doesn't pay to shoot up a roost, incidentally. That can drive the birds completely out of an area, and you'll have to find them all over again.

It's not only doves that are gregarious, but dove hunters also. I don't know any other live-bird shooting sport that puts so many gunners in a given area at the same time, without complaint from any of them. Opening day of pheasant season in southeastern Pennsylvania might show similar numbers, but even those who recognize the others' rights to be there are subconsciously wishing they had the cover to themselves. But in dove shooting, the more the merrier. The reasons are simple: There are enough birds for everyone, and the more gunners around, the more shooting for everyone because they keep the birds moving.

Trying to bag a limit of mourners can be a frustrating experience when you're alone. A picked field can be full of doves, but it's almost impossible to get within range by walking them up. The visibility is so good that they usually flush beyond shooting distance. Once in awhile you'll get a shot—maybe two or three if you're fast—but that's it. The whole flock will be gone, probably to finish feeding at the other end of the field, if it's a big one, or in a different field a mile or so away. If you don't try to get within range of the birds, your only choice is to let them come to you. That means picking a stand they're likely to fly over. Again, if you're the only shooter, the odds are against you, for they have 360 degrees to come in from and you can cover only a fraction of that. Even if you pick a good flight lane, shooting at one bird will often alert other incomers to your position and they simply bend around you.

So results are invariably better when there are enough shooters to cover the flight lanes to a feeding area, and they're best of all when still other shooters have similar setups at other places in the surrounding region. This means that no matter what direction the birds come or go, someone gets shooting. This keeps them moving, and in the normal course of events, everyone will get some chances. Certain stands always seem better than others on a given evening—there's something about the overall conditions that makes doves persist in following a particular flight plan—but even peripheral stands usually do okay when there are birds in the area. It pays to observe the amount of shooting at different locations, though. If one man limits out in a hurry and nobody beats you to it, shift to his stand if things are slow at yours. It doesn't make sense to let a hot position go to waste.

At a large shoot in the South, everyone might be an invited guest of the landowner, who assigns locations, perhaps transports shooters to and from their stands by truck, and in general manages the event. Most of the shooters are probably longtime acquaintances, and new ones are quickly made to feel that way. The air is pleasant, even festive, almost as much a social affair as a shoot. There's a lot to be said for an occasional wingding like this. However, when the banging starts there's not the slightest doubt that the fundamental purpose of the get-together is to shoot doves. The large gatherings of hunters are made possible by the large flocks of birds and made necessary by the large fields in which they're shot, fields sometimes hundreds of acres in extent. Doves like to feed in a certain field on a given evening, so they tend to keep coming in regardless of the shooting. They'll quickly fill their crops at one end of a field while steady shooting is going on at the other, or even come in through the guns, land and commence feeding. If a field is surrounded by shooters, the action will be loud and hectic, so much so, perhaps, that it will eventually prove too much for the doves and they'll leave that area and move to another field. So it is possible to overdo a good thing.

Things are somewhat different in most other dove shooting regions. Feeding areas where I do most of my hunting tend to be smaller, with fewer birds and fewer shooters. And there is less tradition for an invited group of friends to do the honors of an evening. Quite often, shooters around the perimeter of a field or at various stands here and there are complete strangers to each other, their presence being only the result of their common interest in dove shooting. It's not unusual for four or five hunters to park in the same place, take the same stands, and shoot "together" several evenings a week for a couple of months, yet never even learn the others' names. This despite the fact that they often exchange small talk when coming or going, help each other look for downed birds, even offer shells to someone who has run out. I'm not suggesting that either of these setups is better than the other, only that both are normal and that anyone who wants to hunt doves should try it, even if he has no connection with a semi-organized group.

Anyway, when a dove area is located and you have obtained permission to hunt, it's a good idea to arrive somewhat

A few cornstalks conceal a hunter well enough, so long as he remains motionless as doves approach. Movement scares them more than color.

ahead of normal flight hours and get set up. In the Eastern Management Unit, shooting hours are normally from noon until sunset, so what the birds do in the morning is of academic interest only. And since things are slow during midday, there's little point being out there before 3 or 4 PM. At the beginning of the season (the opener is usually September 1), everyone is raring to go, so they're typically in the field, gun loaded, etc., on the stroke of noon. The eagerness tends to slacken a bit as the hours wear on and the sun's heat accumulates, but that's how opening days affect you. Eventually, the mourners start moving, the guns go off, and everything's copacetic again.

Since most hunting is done in the fall, there's an instinctive feeling that the weather should be cool whenever you're in the field with a gun. However, early September is still the tag end of summer, and my dominant memory, looking back over a lot of seasons, is that the weather is sweltering whenever I'm dove shooting. I know that isn't always the case, but I have trouble recalling a cool hunt and none whatsoever conjuring up countless memories of hot days afield. Part of this is due to the too-early starts in the beginning of the season, already explained, and part to the lack of physical action. Most dove shooting requires little movement and there are often considerable periods between shots, so you have lots of time to think about being uncomfortable. It's a valid thought, too. Consider my first hunt of the year, a typical situation.

Being an old experienced dove shooter, one who knows they don't start moving well till 4 PM or so, I didn't even leave the office until 11:30. That way I had time to drive home, eat lunch, change clothes, load my old Jeep with all the necessities and putter my way to the killing grounds. It was actually 1 o'clock when I arrived—a full hour into the new season. That is genuine restraint on opening day! I'd made a mistake, my instincts told me, for five other cars were already parked at a pull-off where a dirt farm road met the blacktop. I was glad there'd be other guys around, but of course believed that they would have the best locations. Such thoughts are second nature to all hunters.

Hurriedly—I didn't want any other latecomers to get ahead of me—I buckled on the shell carrier I use for claybird shooting (it's a handy gadget for dove hunting, as it keeps ammo readily available and also has a pocket to carry empties home for reloading), dumped a box of 20-gauge field loads into it, shoved another box into the pocket of my camouflage jacket,

Dove shooters spend a lot of time looking for downed birds. Mark each one well as it falls and don't take doubles over thick cover unless you have a good retriever.

If caught in the open by incoming birds, stand motionless; they'll probably come on in. Don't raise the gun and aim while waiting. Just flip it up and shoot as they get into normal killing distance. Trying to make sure of a hit by deliberately "putting it on 'em" is the road to missing.

Large dead trees attract doves even without decoys, as they like sitting in high places where they can see well.

tied a blue bandanna loosely around my neck to catch the sweat dribbles and help keep off the gnats, put on the Ray-Bans and my old Stetson, and took off up the dirt road on foot, the Ithaca SKB over the crook of my arm.

The road curved up through a shallow valley, planted to hay, a weedy ditch running alongside the road on the right, low wooded ridges on either side of the valley. It was fairly narrow at first, then broadened out, with assorted small fields showing the remains of tomatoes, cantaloupes, squash, etc., fencerows and thicketed sidehills rising to several small fields of standing corn on top. They too were divided by brambly fencerows, with patches of trees scattered about. It doesn't sound like typical dove country, but they were there. I'd seen 'em earlier. Other hunters had, too, for they were already in position. I hadn't gone 50 yards when I passed the first, ensconced in a little hideaway he'd made in the weedy ditch, comfortable on a folding aluminum seat which also served as a shell carrier. His 1100 Remington stood between his feet, an open box of shells was handy nearby, and he was swigging on a root beer he'd just taken out of a cooler.

"That's the life," I said. He just grinned. I thought of my own cooler back in the Jeep. I'd been so anxious to get started, I hadn't even remembered to stick a can of Coke in my pocket to drink after I got to my stand. But I wouldn't go back now, not for that nor for the folding canvas seat. Going back is unlucky.

On the hillside to the left, I spotted another hunter, and a second in some weeds beneath a walnut tree ahead. And I soon passed two more in rough spots where the valley widened out. These guys knew what they were doing. There was no food, but any birds approaching from the west would be funneled right past the guns in the narrow valley. There was no room for me here, so I followed a thick fencerow toward the cornfields on top, finally taking a stand in a tree-edged opening grown to high grass which was too rough for planting.

I was sweating already and the day had hardly begun. I moved into some shade, wiped my glasses and looked around. Nothing moving. I could see a couple of hunters in a treeline some distance downhill, but there was no action anywhere. Time passed and the sun beat down and I tried to think of a

A portable cooler makes it easy to keep downed doves fresh as well as providing a cold Coke from time to time. Paul Failor always came prepared—note folding chair in background.

cheek than of the report. Two birds were down, the image of their puffing outlines still visible in my mind, tiny feathers floating toward me further proof that I'd connected. I found one easily and spent 10 minutes searching the waist-high brown grass that grew between the rows of corn before I lucked onto the other. ''You shouldn't try for doubles over cover like this,'' I told myself repeatedly during the search. It's easy to lose them both, particularly easy to lose the first one dropped, as even its general location is lost track of when swinging on the second bird. Still, there's always an instinct to shoot so long as game is in sight, and it's debatable if any gunner should try to override his instincts. It could cost him dearly in some situations.

The shooting was good that day, not only for me but for the others I'd seen in the area. I don't know if everyone limited out, but I managed to get 12, though certainly not with 12 shots. I've never done that and never saw anybody do it, though one fellow, an older shooter, tells me he does it every so often. He's a nice old guy and I'd never suggest that he toys with the truth, but somehow I don't believe him. If he does it, he must pass up all of the questionable chances and take nothing but the kind he handles perfectly. Even then I'm not so sure. A dove is so darn small—its vital area can't be much bigger than a baseball—that it can be right in the middle of a pattern at medium range and still not stop a pellet. Sooner or later, even on the duck soup shots, the dove's location is going to coincide with a blank space in the pattern and leave the shooter mumbling even more to himself than usual.

Guns and Gear

You don't need a lot of unusual equipment to go dove hunting, but as suggested in the shoot just described, some items are so useful that they've become almost a uniform for this sport. First, of course, is a camouflage outfit. Unlike most mammals, birds do see colors, so the fluorescent orange hats and vests so popular with big game hunters are seldom

rational explanation for being out so early. There was none. Still, it beat being in the office. I wiped the back of my neck and thought of the Cokes in the cooler in the Jeep. It was scarcely ½-mile away but I couldn't go get one. Something might go over my stand while I was gone. The sky was a pale-blue shimmering bowl, cloudless, reflecting the heat downward like an oven, making me squint even through the dark glasses. I thought I heard a shot, listened harder, did hear one. Then two more. The season was really underway! I searched the sky. It was still empty. I checked my gun again—probably the third time since I'd been there. The heads of the same two shells stared back at me unfeelingly.

I made sure the safety was on, stared out across the field, watching the mirage rise above the corn. Not a breath of air stirred. My camouflage jacket felt as impermeable as plastic. Inside my boots I could feel my toes curling into quivering masses of athlete's feet. Sweat tickled its way through my eyebrows, burned my eyes. I wiped them with a second bandanna—years back I learned to carry several—cleaned my glasses again, then tied the bandanna around my forehead to make a sweatsoaker. I cussed myself for forgetting the Coke and, my lower back aching dully now, for forgetting the folding seat. Walking all day was easy, but just standing brought little nagging problems. I wished it was later. Later, it would be cooler and the birds would be moving. I wished I had a drink. I . . . There they came, four of them, quicksilver streaks just above the corn, angling across so deceptively that it was hard to realize how fast they were going. I swung without thought, the *Boom-Boom* of the little SKB registering on my eardrums as if fired some vast distance away. I was more conscious of the way the stock moved against my sweaty

The late Paul Failor, Lemoyne, Pennsylvania, was an expert hunter, trapper and fisherman, a fine writer and a friend of many years. Here he used a dove call to attract birds.

seen in the weedfields of September. I'm not certain this is all to the good, as you can be just as dead from a close-range misplaced load of 7½s as from a .30-06 bullet, but that's the way it is. Several small patches of orange sewed to the back shoulders of the camo jacket would normally be invisible to incoming birds, yet might keep a gunner to your rear from trying to pick off a low bird crossing between you. Be that as it may, the vast majority of dove hunters wear camouflage. It should be a bit sloppy in size, for easy gun swinging and coolness.

In the early hot weather, some like a mesh vest more than the usual military-style jacket. It's not as concealing in its effect, particularly if you wear a white undershirt, which a lot of unthinking guys do, but it is cool and comfortable unless the bugs are too numerous. Some of these vests have a large game pocket, which is handy for shells or empties and makes it easy to lug along such useful items as insect repellant. I'd sooner be a bit warmer than put up with the annoyance of various insects, so wear a sleeved camo jacket that has two large pockets for assorted items. A lot of shooters always wear camouflage pants, too, but others settle for Levi's or something similar. All seem okay so long as their color is dull and generally blends with the background. The jacket should hang outside the pants to let air circulate. I dislike coveralls because they are in effect a sealed unit, hotter than blazes at this time of year.

I prefer low leather boots to the shoes or sneakers which some guys choose. They're warmer but are more protective in the high weeds where you often hide, or for kicking around in the thick cover where birds often drop. They can be especially important in poisonous-snake country.

A wide-brimmed hat is a lifesaver when you're out in the sun for hours at a stretch. Cowboys knew what they were doing when they developed that style. It doesn't have to be a high quality felt job—lightweight straw ones are readily available and cooler—but it should be a dull, nonreflecting color. The brim not only shields against the sun but also shades the face, which is probably the most visible thing to a bird in the sky, cuts glare, and offers protection for the face and ears when you are kicking around in brambles or standing corn, trying to find a dead dove. If you can't find a dull-colored straw hat in the store, buy what they have and spray paint it in camouflage effect.

Hardened shooting glasses are recommended. They protect the eyes against all sorts of things besides glare—stray shot pellets, for instance. Sure, the odds are great that you'll never have a pellet hit you in the eye, but it only has to happen once to change your life drastically, and perhaps end your shooting days. Medical science can do a helluva lot of wonderful things, but replacing eyes is still beyond them. I once had a gun blow up in my face and spent much of an afternoon having tiny bits of cartridge case brass removed from the surfaces of my eyeballs by an iron-nerved surgeon with a tiny metal pick, so I can tell you firsthand that eye problems can arise while shooting. Instantaneously—with no warning whatsoever. I spent several days after that incident with my eyes bandaged shut, and during a lot of that time I kept thinking that if I'd been wearing good glasses when things let go, they'd have protected me fully from the effects of that particular accident. It's something to keep in mind. It's easier to get a pair of matched Purdeys than a new pair of eyes.

I've already talked about the convenience of a portable seat, shell carrier and bandannas, but I mention them again because they're more important than many shooters realize. It's impractical to sit on the ground during long quiet stretches because you can't get into operation quickly enough when a dove does appear. Also, chiggers can be a problem, and occasionally ants. The shell carrier is faster to reload from

than a pocket when birds are coming fast, and the bandanna has many uses. One is a necessity for wiping your glasses occasionally. A second can be wet with water and folded inside the hat on scorching days, draped from beneath the rear of the hat to protect the neck and ears from gnats or the sun, and even used to wrap your birds into a bundle for carrying to the car if you have no game bag.

A game bag is an oft-forgotten item when dove shooting is new to someone. Traditional hunting jackets have built-in game pockets, but most camouflage jackets don't. A new shooter rarely realizes this until he's faced with the problem of taking care of his birds. They can be tossed in the shade near your stand during the shooting, though they sometimes attract flies. To avoid this, I cover them with pulled grass or, preferably, shove them into a carrier of some sort. The fine mesh bags that potatoes or onions come in at the supermarket make handy dove carriers, as they cost nothing, are lightweight, have a drawstring closure, and they let the air circulate. Do *not* use plastic bags. They are impervious to air and quickly lead to spoilage in typical dove shooting weather. The mesh bag can be looped over your belt for convenience while walking. Or a more durable bag can be sewn up from an odd piece of lightweight canvas. My daughter made me one with a tunnel to slide over the shell carrier belt. It's big enough to hold 12 doves, is less prone to tear than a mesh bag and eliminates the fly problem. When necessary, it can be thrown in the washer and cleaned. And when claybird shooting, it holds four or five times as many empties as the regular carrier. One caution: Sometimes I forget myself while hunting and drop empties into it along with doves. Invariably, feathers will work their way into the cases before I get home. These can be a problem when they're reloaded, so if you try anything like this, be sure to check inside them.

A cooler is a great idea. Styrofoam designs are inexpensive and will serve, though they get broken easily. A metal or heavy plastic style is better over the long haul, and useful on picnics, etc., as well as for hunting. The cooler makes it easy to have a softdrink or some ice water occasionally, and also solves the problem of what to do with dead doves during a long afternoon. This assumes you'll be within reasonable walking distance of the car, as it's not too practical to carry the cooler very far. I prefer to use ice as a cooling agent rather than the commercial stuff that can be refrozen for repeated use. It's refreshing to chew a small piece of ice once in awhile, and you can even wash your hands with it if necessary.

Military ammo boxes make indestructible units for carrying a good supply of shells to your stand. The .50-caliber size holds six boxes of 12-gauge shells, which is enough for you and a buddy even when you're not connecting well, and you can squeeze five boxes of 20s into the .30-caliber (7.62 NATO) size. Both sizes have quick-detachable lids which pressure close on an integral gasket to form a seal that's dustproof and probably waterproof. Put a couple handfuls of shells into your pockets for immediate use, and replace them from the box as needed.

As mentioned earlier, dove hunters rarely construct true blinds but a sturdy pocketknife is helpful in trimming out a cubbyhole in high weeds for a stand. Shooters don't have to be invisible to doves, so long as they don't move when birds are coming in. Often, standing against a utility pole or tree—anything to break up the outline and make tiny movements inconspicuous—is enough of a "blind."

Some hunters use calls and decoys to attract doves. At times, these seem to work. The late Paul Failor of Lemoyne, Pa., seemed to have considerable faith in a good show of decoys, and he certainly took a lot of doves during the years I hunted with him, so maybe there's something to it. However, it's impossible to know if we'd have got similar numbers on

The author examines decoys which Paul Failor will place high in tree to lure in doves. Decoys are placed on a limb with body on one side, weight wire on the other. To be visible from a long distance, decoys must be high in a tree that has some bare limbs.

(Above) The jointed pole is light in weight and can be lengthened to reach into almost any tree. Open metal end makes it easy to lift and install decoys.

(Right) Here, Paul Failor lifts a decoy into a tall walnut. A dozen or more in such a tree will often bring in many targets.

For visibility, dove decoys on the ground should be set in almost-bare areas where they can easily be seen by incoming or passing birds.

those same days if we didn't have decoys out. The thing is, Paul was a great fellow for proper procedures and equipment. For him, it wasn't enough just to do something; it had to be done in what he conceived as the proper way. He greatly enjoyed the months of preparation prior to any hunting season, be it for doves or ducks or deer, and spent many long hours getting equipment into perfect condition for every outing. It was a full blown safari to spend a day in his Susquehanna duck blind, and a dove shoot was almost as big a deal.

Most hunters who use dove decoys fasten a few to low bushes or fences and hope for the best. Paul preferred to get his foolers up high. "It's the natural thing to do," he'd say. "That's where live doves sit and that's where they're visible. You want them to be seen a long ways off, and you want enough of them to create some attraction."

Now, it's impossible to climb a tree and distribute decoys by hand. You can't get them out on the small limbs where live ones sit without risking a broken neck. Paul solved the problem neatly by building a small-diameter jointed pipe to lift them into place while his feet were planted firmly on the ground. He always used full body decoys with a small weight that held them vertical, and when he got through decorating a dead walnut or whatever, it looked like a hunter's Christmas tree. He also placed some on the ground, if it was bare enough for the airborne critters to see them, so it looked as if some were feeding. And as I said, we got doves with such setups, but maybe we'd have got them anyway.

The best decoy trees are obviously those which can be seen for a long ways. It also helps if they're located where ground cover is sparse. Doves like to feed on waste grain, weed seeds, etc., and will sooner come into areas where they can see well than where cover is thick. Another advantage of relatively clear ground is the ease with which downed birds can be found. A dove is an inconspicuous color even in the hand; when it falls dead in a field of standing corn that's also waist high in weeds, it can be devilishly hard to locate. It isn't always possible to have a decoy tree right where you want it, but you should keep the ideal setup in mind. It's common to find a suitable tree in a fencerow between fields. If one field is in tall corn, say, and the other is a meadow or pasture or a harvested field, discipline yourself to shoot birds so they will fall in the open. Similar setups are often available when the landowner is cutting swaths of corn for silage, leaving alternate strips standing. Doves will come in to feed in the cut strips and the shooter can stand just inside the uncut corn, invisible to the birds, and drop them in the open areas.

Retrieving Doves

When shooting over semi-bare fields, it's okay to try for doubles or even triples. (The latter is a rarity for most shooters, but happens occasionally; doubles are fairly common. Either makes a shooter feel good.) However, it's doubtful that anyone should try for more than one bird when shooting over thick cover. Doves fly so fast that by the time you get on the second bird and shoot, it usually falls a considerable distance from the first. You might pinpoint the second one's impact, but finding the first tends to be difficult. Even if you miss the second, you'll already have lost track of the first, so you can end up without getting any. It's best to keep your gaze riveted on the individual bird as it comes down. Mark it by some conspicuous weed or whatever and get it in a hurry. If you can't find it immediately, hang a spare bandanna where you think it hit and move outward in spirals, looking under everything. A dove can disappear under a plantain leaf and cripples will hide if given the chance. They're tougher than they look. If a shot is taken over standing corn or other stuff that all looks alike, it pays to make a habit of estimating the distance from you to the falling bird. The estimate doesn't have to be as precise as 27 or 38 yards or whatever, but you should be able to recall if it was a short shot—20 to 25 yards, say—a medium shot of 35 yards or so, or a long shot of 40 yards or more. Then count your steps as you head right for the last place you saw the bird; chances are you'll be fairly close to it when you've stepped off the appropriate distance.

The ideal item of equipment for finding doves, of course, is a good retriever. If you have one and help him by directions based on the previous suggestions, it's unlikely that he'll miss more than an occasional bird. It's a common belief that dogs don't like to retrieve doves, but I'm not sure that's true. I've hunted with a number of them that willingly found and brought back these small gray hummers. Obviously, the loose

Most dogs dislike retrieving doves because their feathers are so loose that every bird leaves a mouthful behind. But they'll bring them in for you, so take the time to wipe out the dog's mouth and make sure he has plenty of water on the hot days.

feathers can be a nuisance, but it's only a moment's job to wipe them out of the dog's mouth. Most retrievers are intelligent enough to appreciate this and some even indicate they want it done. Don't forget that the dog needs water during the hot days even more than you do. It's dusty as well as hot at his level, as his living parts are closer to the ground than yours. So take plenty of water with you unless you're certain there's a good pond or creek in the shooting area.

The purebred retrievers—I'm partial to Labs as I've had good luck with several—are great on doves, but any kind that will search out and bring back a downed bird is a godsend. Some mixed-breed farm dogs do well at this, seeming to have a built-in urge to find game. They won't all retrieve, but that's a minor flaw if they find the bird. You can always walk over and pick it up. Once in awhile a dog will decide to eat the birds he finds, though, and that's not something a hunter should put up with.

Many dogs become great dove spotters after they've learned what's on the agenda. They'll sit by your stool, watching so intently they're quivering when birds are approaching, and take off like a shot when they see one fall to the gun. Some purists insist that the dog wait for their command to fetch, while others want him to go at the hit, figuring that reduces losses. It probably isn't too important which way the shooter prefers. Doves knocked down in sight of a good retriever are seldom lost.

Since there can be an awful lot of gun noises when doves are flying well and a lot of shooters are out, it's debatable whether a young dog should be subjected to this experience. It makes some of them nervous and confuses others. They sometimes want to retrieve every bird they see fall, even if it's 200 yards away and was dropped by a complete stranger. (That's not necessarily bad unless the pup wants to bring the bird to you, but such minor problems are easily worked out. Once in awhile a stranger is grateful that you've brought a dog.) Many dogs take all the hoopla in stride, reveling in the periodic excitement and earning their keep all the way. In the end, the only way to know how one will react is to try him.

Hints on Hitting

A fellow whose shooting experience has been accumulated on grouse, quail or pheasants can be confused by doves. Most upland game birds are not seen until a few seconds before they're shot at. Even pointed birds are usually hidden from the hunter's view until flushed. As a result, the bird's sudden appearance at short-range is the stimulus to which he reacts by instantaneously mounting his gun and firing. Doves, by comparison, are mostly seen at long-range. Shots are taken on incoming birds, or at birds which are angling past one way or another within shooting distance. The gunner often has his targets in view a rather long time before he has the slightest chance of hitting them. New hunters tend to think this is an advantage, as they can deliberately get the gun up, take good "aim," and really sock it to 'em. The usual outcome of such shooting is a miss. Sometimes two or three, if the gun holds that many shells. There is a deliberateness about the aimed approach to shotgunning that is self-defeating, and it's never more apparent than on doves. The system might work if the shooter constantly reminded himself to swing the muzzle through the bird, and keep it moving, but the vast majority of such shots are taken with a motionless gun, almost as if firing at a bull's-eye from a benchrest. However, the bird is almost never coming right into the muzzle; it's invariably moving at some angle in relation to the gun, usually at a good rate of speed. The net result is a shot charge that passes behind the target. On rare occasion the shooter will be so impressed by the little critter's zippiness as it passes that he gooses that barrel like an International Skeet shooter and actually catches up with the bird and demolishes it. But usually if the first shot goes behind, successive ones do too.

It's far better to wait with the gun in a comfortable carrying position while watching incomers, then swing it up and through the bird's path, firing as you go, in the same time period a flushing bird would get. That way there's no hesitation or attempt to get a perfect aim or freezing up at the critical moment. You just react and shoot. And hit.

But don't wait too long to react. To get the best performance out of your shell—pattern size and density—you ought to take incomers about 30 yards in front of you. However, a dove cruising straight in at 40mph is getting about 60 feet closer every second. If you take a second to flip the gun up and fire, he'll be 20 yards closer when the shot goes off than when you reacted. So don't wait until he's within 30 yards before you decide to shoot. If you do hit him, you'll kill him all right—so thoroughly that nothing edible will be left—but your pattern will be so small you're more likely to miss. Learn to react when an incomer reaches 40 yards or so, and hit him at about 30.

Swing from behind on all birds and shoot when the muzzle passes the head. Do this even on doves coming right over your position. On such shots, swing up from below and fire when the bird disappears behind the muzzle. It's sort of odd to shoot at something you can't see, but on this kind of incomer that's the only way you'll connect.

Sometimes a dove will get almost overhead before you see it. There's no way you can catch up with such a target while facing the way it came. If you rapidly turn around to face the direction it's flying, you might be able to take it going away. For such shots you fire when there's 6 inches or so of space between the top of the muzzle and the bird, a shot that's very similar to the high house station one Skeet bird.

Because quite a few hunters often congregate in a relatively small area for dove shooting, safe gun handling becomes even more imperative than usual. It's quite easy to send a shot down a fenceline when a bird darts through an opening between a couple of tall trees, but that's a dangerous shot to take. Fencelines are often used as natural blinds, which means you can be endangering other hunters by any low shot you fire in that direction. Even if certain no one is in the fencerow itself, low shots are bad for they can pepper or seriously hurt someone as much as several hundred yards away, out of sight. It's best to make a habit of shooting doves only at a steep upward angle. The pellets are going to come to earth somewhere, of course, but will be falling only with a velocity due to gravity, and they are such light objects, individually, that they have little energy. I've been sprayed with falling pellets on occasion, but hardly noticed it. I've never heard of anyone being injured by such shot, but it's always best to wear hardened shooting glasses to protect the eyes.

For some reason, few dove articles talk about walking up doves as a hunting method. They describe pass shooting on birds going to or from feeding areas, water or roosts, but largely ignore this more active method whereby the hunter goes to the birds instead of vice versa. Admittedly, this isn't a popular system, but occasional birds can be taken this way. It's usually tried when few birds are flying and the shooter gets tired of watching the heat waves curl up off the fields and mopping the sweat off the back of his neck. Any kind of action seems preferable to the endless waiting, so eventually most dove hunters do a little hiking through the thicker cover.

It's often claimed that doves do their feeding in open fields, preferring to pick seeds off ground that is nearly bare. That's common of course. However, anyone who will take the time to wander through various kinds of cover will learn that doves often feed in fields of standing corn where the tassels are 4 feet above your head and the ground cover is hip-high weeds you can barely plow through. They also feed in stubble, cantaloupe, pumpkin or squash fields which have grown up in weeds. Obviously they can't see well when in such fields—a supposed requisite for feeding areas—but nevertheless they're there.

The problem is to get within gun range of these birds. Even if they can't see you, it's apparently not difficult to hear or sense your movement as you plow through the shrubbery, so they rather consistently take flight when you're still a few yards out of sure shotgun effectiveness. Fast gun work will sometimes drop a dove, and on rare occasions a pair of them, though a double brings the problem of finding the downed birds. Shooting is probably toughest when moving within standing corn, as flushed birds flicker in and out of sight as if passing on the other side of a picket fence. They vanish quicker than birds kicked out of weedfields even though they may be closer when they leave the ground. But no matter what kind of cover they go out of, walked-up birds tend to leave a bit before you'd like them to and they depart at their normal speed—fast! So you gotta get on them fast.

You also have to keep an eye out for passing birds, at least when working through a weedfield. Deep in a cornfield, nobody is likely to get shooting at birds accidentally passing by, but outside, where visibility is better, incomers can often be seen while still in the distance. Stand motionless if there's a chance a dove will come within range. If it does, shoot as if it's coming in to the blind you deserted to try your luck on foot.

Occasional shots will be offered if you slowly parallel a fencerow or treeline that divides some fields. Doves commonly sit in such trees, or along the edges of woods, and a fast shooter will drop some when his approach routs them out. Doves also like to hang out in orchards, but most owners are reluctant to let shooters into these areas. They don't want fruit-bearing trees riddled by numerous shot charges—an understandable feeling considering the sloppy way some shooters operate. A sensible hunter who talks to an orchard owner, identifies himself properly so the owner knows he can find him if anything bad happens, and shows he's aware of the possible problems and knows how to avoid them, can sometimes get permission to shoot where no one else is allowed. It takes personal effort to get into such places, but it can be worth it.

Taking a few doves in places like these can be interesting just because they're different. Once in awhile they provide a shot that's different too. For instance, a few seasons back I was idly working my way through a good size field of osage orange when I happened to glance around just in time to see a high dove angling across in a path that would take it in front of the sun. Without conscious thought I snapped the little 20-gauge Winchester 101 up, fired—and watched a sparkling silver halo appear as a cloud of feathers erupted against the bright blue sky. And then, to compound the incident, the dove never came down. It was dead, all right, an instant kill, but it arced downward in a graceful fall only to strike in the top of a tall dead tree that was overgrown with dense green creepers. There was no way for me to get that bird. The best Lab in the country could not have retrieved it for me. But I remember it far more clearly than most of those I've brought home through the years.

Yes, the dove does supply some surprises. I guess that should be expected from the only game bird in the country that weighs less than the shot charges it takes to down him.

CHAPTER 6

Bobwhite Quail

THE BOBWHITE IS another one of those birds which hold a special place in the hearts of hunters. In fact, throughout most of the South, the term "bird hunting" refers only to hunting the bobwhite quail. More than a few locals doubtless lived their entire lives without learning that the "bird" they hunted every fall was actually a quail . . . and they wouldn't have attached any importance to it one way or the other if someone had told them so. After all, what's in a name. The important thing is the bird itself, and the dogs, and the guns, and maybe one good hunting buddy. Yes, the bobwhite is something special, and those who favor this lovely little rocket just gaze at you with a look reserved for idiots if you happen to suggest that the ruffed grouse—or, God forbid, the ringneck—might be this country's top game bird.

The bobwhite is a pretty small critter to arouse such emotion. Full-grown, he's well under a foot in length, including a short tail, and an adult's weight averages about 6 ounces, with occasional birds reaching 8 or 9 ounces. The head is small and round, and wings are short and rounded. In fact, that's the overall impression given by this bird—roundness or chunkiness. He doesn't fly in a chunky style, though. From a standing start, usually invisible among the ground cover, he reaches full speed in an instant, whirring his way toward the nearest cover like a dirty tennis ball blasted out of an oversize air gun. When a large covey takes off like this, maybe 15 birds going out simultaneously, it makes for an interesting moment or two, and helps explain the attraction these little birds have for gunners.

The bobwhite, *Colinus virginianus,* isn't our only quail, but it's the only one thought of as an eastern quail. It occurs almost exclusively east of the Rockies, and notably in the Southeast, though a few have been stocked in the Pacific Northwest. The five other quail species native to this country, the California, Mountain, Gambel's, Scaled and Harlequin, are western birds, primarily southwestern. There are four or five subspecies of the bobwhite, but the differences are mostly apparent to scientific types only. They all look pretty much alike over the end of a gun barrel—which is to say, chestnut-brown plumage with white and black markings on top, and creamy underparts having dark bars. The male has a white throat and eyeline divided by a dark brown band, giving him a comparatively conspicuous head; the female is buff colored instead of white here, with a light brown divider. Some gunners have eyes and reactions sharp enough to let them select and shoot only cockbirds on a covey flush, but this takes considerable experience and concentration.

The bobwhite gets his popular name from his call, a whistled *bob-white* He also makes a subdued clucking at times, and there is a soft assembly call, *purr-leer, purr-leer,* used when members of a broken covey are trying to get back together. Bobwhites are social birds and function largely as a covey, the members feeding together and loafing in the same area. The unit has a home range of about 10 to 100 acres, wandering only up to 1/4-mile or so daily, if not greatly disturbed. At night the covey roosts together, squatting in a circle, tails together and heads pointing outward. This helps maintain body heat and makes it difficult for a predator to approach undetected.

Coveys break up in the spring as the mating urge comes on them. This is fortunate from any viewpoint, as there is a high mortality rate on this species—about 75 percent annually, no matter whether they are hunted or not—so it's time to rebuild the population. More males than females survive the winter, and since bobwhites are monogamous this means that some males will not be able to find mates. Thus there is considerable competition for available females, and the cockbirds put on courtship displays that include strutting with puffed-out plumage and fanned tails, and singing. Occasionally there is fighting, but this isn't too serious. Eventually the birds pair off. They build a nest—nothing elaborate, just a depression in some weeds or grass, perhaps in a fencerow or along a creekbank—and the hen begins to lay her eggs, at the rate of about one per day. As many as 10 to 20 have been noted in a clutch, but 14 to 16 is more typical. Incubation takes 23 days. It is usually by the hen and begins after the last egg is laid, thus they all hatch on the same day. If the eggs are destroyed by predators, fire or whatever, the pair will usually renest, but once a brood is produced it is rare for a hen to lay again in the same season.

Chicks weigh scarcely 1/4-ounce when they leave the egg. They are precocial and develop rapidly, though for some weeks they are brooded by the parents during bad weather. They can fly a little at 2 weeks of age and at 4 months are adult size. Orphaned chicks are commonly adopted by other adult pairs. Family groups stay together during the summer, then break up in the fall to assemble later into winter coveys. A lot of them don't make it that far. The world is full of critters which prey on both eggs and chicks—the usual predators such as skunks, snakes, foxes, stray housecats, etc.,—and of course cold rains, prolonged droughts and other acts of nature take their toll. Nevertheless, by fall most areas which can support quail have about as many as can be expected. In the end, the amount of available food and cover determine the population of this, and every other, species. Despite their high reproductive potential, which can mean lots of birds in summer, the basic question is, how many birds can a given area support in February and March? That's when the real crunch comes. It's the time when nature limits a given popula-

A patchwork of tall hay-meadowed areas, pasture grasses, and second-growth woods, Callaway Gardens' 1,000-acre Georgia game preserve is a favorite among sporting enthusiasts. From October through March, visitors can hunt for quail on these well-known grounds with dogs and guides furnished.

tion. So long as there is enough breeding stock alive in the spring, a species will make it through another year. The same principle applies to all critters, but it seems more obvious with quail for some reason, probably because this is a fair-size bird yet most individuals do not survive a full calendar year.

Besides making the countryside more pleasant simply by their presence—it's always delightful to hear bobwhites whistling in the early morning or late afternoon hours, and they're lovely little birds to see taking dust baths or pecking for grit along the edge of a country road—these are very useful creatures. Bobwhites eat countless insects in the summer, the chicks especially benefiting from this source of protein which is invaluable to their rapid growth, and the older birds consume all kinds of weed seeds—foxtail, ragweed, pokewood, pigweed, etc. They also eat berries, nuts, waste grain, greens, and small wild fruits. They sort of follow the seasons with their diet, eating what is available, as any wild creature must do, and surviving on it. But the destruction of vast numbers of Japanese and June beetles, grasshoppers, crickets, cinch and squash bugs, potato beetles, centipedes, snails, sowbugs, etc., is helpful to farmers as well as themselves.

Clean farming practices are hard on quail. They like abandoned fields, grasslands, "open" brush, some pinelands and woods, mixed vegetation, thick fencerows, honeysuckle, greenbriars and weedy areas. A "modern" farmer who wipes out all such cover and utilizes every square foot of land for money crops, one whose fields look as if they were planned with an electronic calculator and laid out with a surveyor's transit, is never going to know the quiet happiness that a whistled *bob-white, bob-white* can bring of a morning. Conversely, the slightly less businesslike landowner who realizes there's more to life than pure efficiency can take a more relaxed approach to things. He leaves some fencerows and brushpiles, some odd corners of brushy weeds, maybe plants a few strips of soybeans, lespedeza or millet nearby, occasionally leaves some grain crops unharvested—not much; it doesn't take much—and ends up with the best of all possible worlds, a farm that not only produces traditional crops but a wildlife crop as well. In this case it's quail, but with slightly different preparations it could be most anything indigenous to a region, for the survival or extermination of wildlife depends on habitat, and man largely controls that now.

Quail hunting can be as simple or as sophisticated as anyone wants—or can afford—to make it. At the one extreme are the vast private areas where perhaps 10 or 15 thousand acres of land are managed for the primary purpose of providing the best possible bird shooting for the owners and their guests. The complement of such a plantation often includes trained wildlife managers, dog trainers and handlers, kennels full of outstanding pointers and setters, with an occasional retriever for finding what the blue-blooded pointing dogs sometimes disdain to bring back, riding horses and tack, four-wheel-drives that have been extensively altered to comfortably accommodate several friends in tailored togs and snakeproof boots, dog boxes, English doubles, shells, refreshments, what have you. The objective isn't ostentation; it's just that there's no other practical way to hunt all those acres, and what's the good of having the land and the birds if you can't hunt them? And so, with a driver who finds it no difficult chore to maneuver the Jeep through the vast fields and open woods, you follow one pair of dogs after another as they move like perfectly programmed machines through the pines and milo and lespedeza. How long one brace will go depends largely on the temperature, but there's always another pair waiting and eager so that's no problem. When one dog slams to a halt, locked up and quivering, and the second honors beautifully, the shooters disembark, unrack and load their guns, and move in.

This, of course, is the sophisticated approach, the South's version of the old-time African safari. There's a lot to be said for this kind of hunting, and probably 'most everyone would like to try it at least once.

At the other extreme is the kid in dusty bluejeans who walks out the kitchen door, grabbing a cut-down single barrel as he goes, whistles up a slat-ribbed pointer from under the porch, and heads for the nearest brushfield.

In between those two extremes lie most of the country's quail hunters, those gunnermen who are interested only in the makings of a delicious meal, the specialists who see the bobwhite as the greatest smoothbore challenge in the world, and all those who hunt this little buzzbomb for other reasons of their own, perfectly simple or highly complex. To further their own success, they study the bird, its habits, its habitat, its way of life. They note that birds move to feed in early morning and late afternoon, doing their loafing and dusting in the midday hours. So early and late are the best times to hunt them. The birds' movements leave scent for the dogs to find, and this is easier to do when the dew has not been sucked up by the sun or blown away by rising winds. They also note that

today's birds almost invariably head for thick cover when flushed, rarely landing in an open field even if kicked out of one. Increased hunting pressure over the last few decades has brought this defensive move about. Today's birds are the descendants of those which survived previous seasons and the survivors are the ones which made it toughest for the hunter. Thick cover makes shots tougher. They note that the shooting is quick, the ranges short, so a light, fasthandling gun using a reasonable charge of fine shot is obviously the ticket. Most end up with an ounce of 7½s or 8s, with a few going to 9s, and quite often these loads are stuffed into a gas-operated 20-gauge autoloader. This design seems to kick less than any other and it has the three-shot capability which at least makes it possible to think in terms of a triple—something that's not too likely with a double gun, no matter how skilled the shooter.

"Pointers"—the Quail Hunter's Dog

Most all quail hunters conclude, sooner rather than later, that for any reasonable success they've got to have dogs. It's possible to kill occasional quail without a dog, but no one would expect to do it consistently. Birds bagged this way are usually accidental shots taken while hunting other game. An example occurred a couple of seasons back when John Behel and I were hunting pheasants near Gettysburg. Southeast Pennsylvania has a few quail, but they were the last thing on my mind as we worked along a low, chopped-off sidehill. We had just altered direction and I was making the wide swing when I heard a muffled whirring from John's direction. I looked around in time to see a scramble of small birds that had gone out at his feet. They had only a short distance to go before vanishing into a wide thick fencerow, but John's 1100 Remington came up in one smooth movement, went *Boom-Boom-Boom,* and three bobwhites puffed up into larger balls and dropped motionless. It was an honest-to-God triple, a beautiful example of instinctively reacting to unexpected game and handling a smoothbore the way it was

Reverend John Frehn has hunted quail in several states each season for many years, usually takes 150-200 annually with his pet Model 12 Winchester ... and then stocks that many the following year. He's a real expert with his old slide action. (Photo by Ted Godshall.)

meant to be done. I'll remember that shooting as long as I live, and I'm sure John will, too.

That example was one of the exceptions to the rule, but no one will disagree that for regular success on bobwhites you've got to have dogs. It wouldn't be sensible to say you need a dog more than a gun (you can't shoot anything without a gun), but for all practical purposes you can't shoot quail without a dog, either. This is the bird for which the pointing dog was created. And so anyone who thinks of himself as a quail hunter—anyone who *is* a quail hunter—somehow has access to a pointing dog or dogs. The serious hunters have their own, if it's at all within the realm of possibility. It just seems more fitting, somehow, than borrowing or hunting with someone else all the time, or scrounging.

Usually it's a pointer. Various breeds have been used on bobwhites, and probably individuals of all kinds have worked out all right, but why mess with the oddball stuff? The pointer has been bred through many generations to find this little bird, and that's what he does, better than any other animal on earth. Charley Dickey probably summed it up better in a few sentences than anyone else could do in a book. It was late at night and a couple of us writer types were in Charley's room in a motel in Georgia or Florida or somewhere—I don't remember exactly where and it doesn't much matter anyhow—and the talk had turned to birds and dogs and guns, as it always does, and someone ventured the opinion that the setter was a good bird dog. Charley sorta studied this guy a bit, then after a sip of whatever it was we were sippin' politely agreed that the setter was quite often a fine bird dog. "Ah've hunted with many a good setter," he said. "Lovely dogs, some of' em." He obviously didn't want to hurt anyone's feelings. "But Ah'll tell you fellas sumthin'," he added, unable to leave things where they might be misunderstood. "When it comes to really findin' birds, a pointer's what you want. A pointer is just a goddam' rough-butted quail huntin' machine!" I guess that's another one of Charley's Laws.

Dogs—pointers and setters and maybe some others—have been bred to their high point of perfection because the quail allows it. This is a predictable bird, at least when compared to the ringneck or even the grouse. When a racing pointer suddenly skids to a halt, twisted into a "C" by a scent no human can savor, and locks up so rigidly that every muscle is quivering like a plucked bow string, you are so certain there's game ahead of that black muzzle that your heart wants to pound its way through your ribs. And you are usually right. The quail is not only a delightful bird and a challenging target and a wonderful meal, he is also honest. His scent says he's there, the dog says he's there, and he is there. The bird made the dog and the dog made the hunter. Together, in the minds of some who mean absolutely nothing sacrilegious, these three form a minor trinity.

And this is the time when each hunter faces his own small moment of truth. No matter how he got there—in an elaborate chauffeur-driven four-wheel-drive, on horseback, or via his own dusty boots, no matter whether he's carrying a short-chambered Purdey double custom tailored to his personal specifications, a 28-gauge 1100 Remington auto, or a chopped-down single barrel Iver Johnson—from this moment on, he is on his own. He must put a shell, or two or three, into whatever gun he is carrying. His own two feet must take him up past that motionless-yet-one-thousand-percent-alive hunting machine that has done its job and now is waiting for the gunner to do his. He must kick out the covey that's still invisible in the low ground cover. And then he must try to hit

This pair of eager pointers knows just what is expected of them and soon will be locked up on the covey that's bound to be waiting not too far away. Then it will be up to the gunner to do his bit. (Photo by Tom Brakefield.)

at least one of those tawny machinegun bullets before they all disappear three microseconds from now in an incredible flurry of sound and dust and motion . . .

It's impossible, he thinks. No one can do it. Alone, maybe, but alongside of a new hunting pardner . . . God. His throat is parched, his chest feels wrapped in rubber bands, his heart is slamming in his ears. He doesn't feel his boots scuffing through the weeds but he can smell the dust. Out of the corner of his eye he glimpses Jerry moving up on the other side, so cool, so relaxed. Why can't he be like that? The side of his forefinger lies against the Remington's safety, the muzzle is out ahead. He's automatically moving in a shooting approach now, left foot forward, right one coming up behind, almost a dance-step—yeah, the Two-Step Quail Waltz, maybe he can start a fad, maybe . . . Jeezus, there they go! A thousand of 'em all directions! Everything is violent blurred motion, there's a wrenching of the gun, a crazy swinging, eyes straining to focus, the sound of distant booming, then . . . it's over.

"Great!" Jerry calls. "You got a pair, I saw your second one fall just past mine." The dog is already bringing one back.

"Yeah, I guess we didn't do too bad," he says. "Nice covey, a dozen birds, at least. I thought for just a second I might get the third one, but I wasn't fast enough."

"That takes some doin'. I haven't made a triple all season."

"Me, neither. Well, one of these days." He smooths his birds' feathers, pockets them, reloads the little Remington and looks out across the weedfield where the pointer is already searching out a single.

CHAPTER 7

Squirrel

SQUIRRELS ARE RIFLE GAME. Sure, I know that untold numbers of them are bagged by shotgunners each year, and I don't criticize anyone for using a smoothbore on a bushytail scrambling through the shagbark tops like an acrobat with itching powder in his jockstrap, or even for loosing a load of 6s at one skittering through the dry oak leaf carpet like a crazy cottontail. Such shots are tough by any standards, and a hunter, particularly if he's primarily out for birds but happens onto a big gray squirrel, is fully justified in using whatever gun

When a squirrel is scrambling through the leafy treetops, no one is going to hit it with a rifle bullet except by pure luck. Nick Sisley would rather put his faith in a heavy load of No. 6 shot and here he shows why he feels that way.

he has in hand at the moment. Still and all, the man who leaves the house with the avowed intention of collecting the makings for a flakey hot squirrel potpie oughta be lugging a rifle. Or maybe, if he wants to really earn his dinner, a handgun. The thing is, those fast difficult shots for which a shotgun is sporting rarely occur on a true squirrel hunt. Most are the result of a noisy approach intended to flush a pheasant or kick out a rabbit. You don't hunt squirrels that way. At least not with a rifle, assuming you expect to get any.

The squirrel is to the upland hunter what the woodchuck is to the summer rifleman—a small, wary target that can be extremely difficult to see, even more difficult to get within range of, and tough enough to require exact bullet placement for the quick clean kill which all sportsmen want. Furthermore, besides matching the chuck as a difficult target, the squirrel is better eating, perhaps the tastiest meat in the woods. All in all, he adds up to a worthwhile target, one that not enough hunters deliberately pursue.

Squirrels are members of the *Rodentia* order, which includes a lot of ground dwellers such as the woodchucks, chipmunks and prairie dogs. Some of these are interesting game animals themselves, but here we're concerned only with the tree squirrels, primarily the gray, *Sciurus caroliniensis*, and the fox, *Sciurus niger*. A smaller cousin, the red squirrel or chickaree, occasionally is shot by a young hunter anxious to bag something. I've never known anyone who ate red squirrels, but have heard it's done.

There is a noticeable difference in sizes among these three. The fox squirrel is by far the largest, averaging about 1½ pounds for adults, with an occasional fat old-timer reaching 2½ or possibly 3 pounds. By comparison, the average adult gray will go about 1 pound, and it will take an awfully big red squirrel to weigh ½-pound. The fox squirrel's length reaches 2 feet, half of which is accounted for by his impressive orange tail. This is about 4 inches longer than the average gray, also including its lovely silver-gray tail. The red is about a foot long, overall.

Most fox squirrels are a reddish-gray on top and pale orange or brownish underneath. They are reasonably quick in movement, but lack the electric reactions of the gray. The basic color of the gray squirrel of course is gray, but there is often a silverish cast to it, and the broad thick tail is edged with this lighter trim. Its underparts are a light gray, often appearing to have a bluish cast. Casual observation suggests that grays are either motionless as a stone statue or dashing away at blistering speeds. Actually, they often are seen moving at a sort of slow lope, almost hesitating between successive jumps, but this is unimpressive compared with their usual super-energetic activity, so it doesn't attract much attention.

Don and Helen Lewis with a couple of Tioga County bushytails. Hers, taken with a Remington 541S, is black—not uncommon in northcentral Pennsylvania.

Wilbur Anderson prefers to do his squirreling in the winter, and he does all right with his pet Remington.

In the more northern regions, black gray squirrels (if that isn't a contradiction in terms) are often seen. For years they've been common in northcentral Pennsylvania, where they make a somewhat unusual trophy for visiting hunters. In fact, I've known one or two persons who made it a point to collect and have mounted a fox, gray, red and "black" squirrel. This does make an interesting little group. Albino squirrels are less common than the melanistic phase, but they do appear. In fact, for the past 12 years or so, we've occasionally seen albino grays—entirely snow white animals—in our backyard. Those that I've seen close-up had the pink eyes of true albinos. They are striking in appearance. At times I've been tempted to collect one, and I actually might try it if I saw such a squirrel in conventional hunting territory, but it doesn't seem an acceptable thing to do so close to home.

Fox squirrels also vary in coloration. They can be yellow or orange or buff color below, some are gray or black with white ears, some tails tend toward white, etc. "Etc.," of course, is a preposterous term when it comes to describing an animal's color, but in this case it's reasonably acceptable since the variations are so extreme. The chickaree is a less complex critter: He's a rusty red on top, gray-white below.

Fox squirrels are found from Rhode Island west to the Dakotas, south to the Gulf of Mexico and east to the Atlantic. Some near relatives are found in various oak regions of the West, from Mexico to the Pacific Northwest. Generally speaking, this big squirrel likes open timber, small stands of large trees, even open country, though in the South they are often found in thick swamp areas. This seeming contradiction adds interest for a hunter, for it lends variety and thus challenge to the species.

Grays are found in generally the same regions as fox squirrels, plus the upper New England states and much of Pennsylvania, where the fox is absent. The gray is by nature a denizen of the deep woods, and in earlier days was unbelievably numerous in the chestnut, oak and hickory forests of the East. Those vast stretches are now gone, yet there are still many wooded areas, and the gray squirrel still thrives there. Not only in the big woods, but also in the smaller woodlots near suburban tracts as well as in rural regions. Conditions which once made it possible for a half-dozen riflemen to kill

In days gone by, squirrel dogs were more often used than now. Results tended to be good, as this old photo by Bill Britton shows.

Target rifles and scopes aren't necessary for good results on squirrels. Most rifle hunters use lightweight guns and "22 scopes," and have little reason to complain. Such outfits are especially popular with young hunters who often don't have the money for fancy rifles.

several thousand grays in a week no longer exist, but it's still possible to bag half a dozen in a day. If that sounds puny by comparison—well, it is, if you measure hunting success only by numbers. But if success for you is seen in terms of doing a difficult thing perfectly several times in one day—by quality rather than quantity shooting, that is—then today's squirrel hunting is still one of the outdoorsman's finest experiences.

Some authorities say gray squirrels breed as early as January, while others believe this doesn't occur until spring. The gestation period is 44 days, the average litter is four or five, and a second litter is not unusual the same year. The young leave the nest—a cavity in a tree or a leafy nest constructed among high branches—at about 6 weeks of age, but stay with

the mother until full grown. Fox squirrels mate in December or January and the gestation period is about 42 days. The usual litter is two to five and the young leave the nest at 6 to 12 weeks of age. In colder regions, one litter per year is normal; sometimes there are two litters in more southern parts of the range.

Numbers of squirrels are often seen in the same area, even the same tree. There is little conflict between them either within the same species or the different species. No one disputes this in regard to the gray and fox varieties, but there long has been a belief that red squirrels castrate young male grays. The idea probably developed from a hunter watching one squirrel chasing another, as they often do, more in playfulness than in conflict, and then shooting a gray which appears to be castrated. However, the male squirrel's testes do not descend into the scrotum until sexual maturity is attained, and occasionally they are retracted after the breeding season has ended. In appearance, these animals might seem castrated, but in reality they are not.

Nuts are the number one item on the squirrel's list of preferred food, be he fox or gray. Hickory nuts probably top all choices, if available, with black walnuts, pecans, white oak acorns, black oak acorns, pig nuts, beechnuts, hazel nuts and field corn forming important parts of their diet also. Fruits, berries, and buds are eaten early in the year, wild cherries being a special favorite in summer. Birds' eggs and fledgling birds also are eaten. Bark, twigs and dormant insects will be utilized in winter. Water is obtained from any available source, including dew and snow, or simply from the plants they eat.

Squirrels do not hibernate; as a consequence, they need food all winter long. In fall they feed prodigiously to accumulate body fat to help them through the cold season, but their most important solution to the daily problem of survival is the food they've buried during fall. At this time of year they constantly cut more nuts and acorns than they can eat, this surplus being buried for the time of severe need that's coming. When late fall weather naturally drops mast (food) from the trees, squirrels take advantage of this and redouble their planting efforts. With nut in the mouth, the front paws are used to dig a hole several inches deep into which the nut is

Only super-dedicated squirrel hunters carry heavy equipment such as this Savage/Anschutz. They pay the price—in money, weight and bulk—because they like the results.

thrust; it is then covered and the dirt tamped down. Usually only one nut is buried in a hole. A single squirrel can bury a thousand or more nuts in a fall, and the animal's excellent sense of smell leads him to this food when he needs it. Nevertheless, there's no doubt that many such plantings never are recovered and eaten, with the result that countless nut trees now exist because decades ago squirrels planted their seeds.

My Favorite Squirrel Gun

Back at the beginning of this chapter I said that squirrels are rifle game, despite the fact that millions are taken annually with shotguns. To get the latter out of the way at once, the simplest thing to suggest if you're going to use a smoothbore is use one as much like a rifle as possible. That is, a tightly choked outfit that will throw a close pattern of 6s. The target is small and often must be taken at fairly long range, so best results will come from the combination that has the best chance of putting a couple of pellets into a vital area that's half the length and no deeper than the corncob that supplied this critter's last meal . . . which is to say, about 1x4 inches. That takes in the brain, neck and forward part of the body where a quick kill can be expected if a solid hit occurs. A more open choke will make hits easier on fast-moving squirrels; however, at long-range open chokes often fail to get enough pellets into the animal for instantaneous results. In the end, I'd prefer a full choke and 1¼ ounces of 6s if deliberately going squirrel hunting with a shotgun. That's something I've never done, though, despite the fact that I've been killing squirrels since 1938. The ones I've shotgunned—and there have been quite a few over the years—were incidental targets taken during pheasant or grouse hunts.

I learned early that squirrels make great targets for rifle-

Some squirrel hunters get involved with more rifles than others, of course. These are some that Don Lewis has used over the past few years. From left to right: Remington 581 with Weaver V22 3x6; Marlin's 39A with a Marlin 3x7; Winchester's 320 with the Weaver D-4; the Ruger 10-22 with a Redfield 4x Westerner; Savage 65 with Weaver B-4; Weatherby XXII with W/B 4x; the Mossberg 340BC with a Weaver B-6; the Savage/Anschutz 64 with the Unertl 1-inch 6x; Ithaca's 49 with a Western Field 4x; and Hi-Standard P1011 with a Weaver C-6.

Milt Anderson of Greenock, Pennsylvania, is another serious squirrel hunter who recognizes the value of good equipment. His pet outfit is a 521T Remington with 6x Unertl target scope. (Photo by Don Lewis.)

men. Dad had a habit of giving me guns for presents—a Daisy air rifle for my fourth birthday, a Crosman .22-caliber pellet gun for my sixth, a M71 Winchester .348 for a high school graduation present, etc. The most significant one, in terms of small game, was the M72 Winchester .22 he gave me for my 12th birthday. It had an adjustable peep sight that made for easy zeroing in and accurate shooting, and a tubular magazine that held a handful of Long Rifle hollow points (I preferred Super-X high speeds in those days; the name just *sounded* deadly . . . and they were), and half again as many Shorts, which I shot up by the bucketful 'cause I could get lots more shooting for the same amount of money.

By the following fall I'd somehow saved enough money to get a Weaver M29-S scope mounted. That wasn't an easy thing to do, late in the Depression. Suddenly, I was king of the hill among the riverbank gang. Everyone had a gun in those days, but I was the only one with a scope, and I zeroed it in at 50 yards with the Super-X loads, carefully following the directions which the late Col. Townsend Whelen so kindly gave a 12-year-old kid when he earlier advised me to get the 29-S. Looking through that little glass was like looking into a new shooting world. By today's standards, it wasn't much of a scope, but I could aim at indistinct targets with a precision that the best of iron sights couldn't match, and if the adjustments didn't meter consistently, and eye relief was limited, and the field of view not too big . . . well, these were limitations I didn't even realize existed then. I *could* zero in, and once zeroed I didn't go much for fooling around with the windage and elevation knobs back then; what I did do was shoot stuff. Cans and other containers, on dumps and thrown into the air, twigs off tall trees, tiny stones, frogs, countless sparrows and starlings, occasionally other birds, once in awhile a rabbit (rarely, one running; who said that field was too small?) or a crow, and later what proved to be the big game for this little gun—gray squirrels.

Squirrels weren't the biggest or toughest game to fall to the M72. That distinction went to woodchucks. But although I killed a fair number of the big marmots with the .22 rimfire, stalking as close as possible and doing my utmost to place the hollow point slug with a mechanical draftsman's precision, I always had the feeling that my outfit was over-matched by these tough targets. At 60 yards a young chuck could be killed almost instantly with a high lung or center-of-the-shoulder shot; it would just sort of stiffen, then slowly collapse, the tail sometimes jerking spasmodically at the end. The 10- or 12-pound old-timers sometimes had too much vitality for such placement. They often got into their holes, doubtless to die, but not quickly. It took a brain shot from the .22 rimfire to anchor a big chuck reliably, and I became reluctant to use the .22 on them. What I wanted for chucks then was a .218 Bee. Meanwhile, the little M72 seemed near perfect on the gray squirrels that dwelt on the wooded ridges and often were seen in the buttonwoods and birches along the river. It had all the accuracy needed for consistent hits, and the power seemed perfectly matched to the quarry.

Take a "Rest"

By then I was learning something about proper shooting methods at a local gun club which had four-position league competition. But not all of this training carried over into the squirrel woods. A tight sling in a solid prone position is great for certain kinds of shots, but rarely usable on bushytails. In fact, I've never had the opportunity to try this one on squirrels. At the other extreme, the offhand position was quick and easy to use, but its limitations were evident—bad enough on paper, where a bad shot just meant lost points, and far worse on game, where it could leave a crippled animal in its tree den to die a lingering death. A practical field position obviously had to be something between these two extremes.

I soon reached the same conclusion that most good rifle

56

hunters come up with: A makeshift rest is the deadliest shooting aid normally available. Some hunters decry such a solution, claiming everyone should "stand on his hind feet and shoot like a man." That's a crock. Save it for the indoor gallery competition. A paper target doesn't bleed and hurt from a jerked shot. Game animals deserve to be hunted by the rules, be killed instantly, and be properly cleaned and taken home for the table. Utilizing whatever kind of a rest will make this possible is the best way to shoot.

In the squirrel woods, it's easy to select a stand which will offer support for the rifle when it's time to shoot. The hunter almost always sits with his back to a tree. The tree breaks up his outline and gives some support, which is restful. However, when game is seen, he suddenly realizes he has no rest for his rifle. Sure, he probably can get into a solid sitting position, elbows locked over knees with the sling helping steady things, and this is far better than trying an offhand shot from a wobbly standing position. But after awhile it might dawn on him that if he had sat *behind* the tree it would have offered great concealment and also provided support for the rifle when the shot was taken. And even later he might realize that the best solution is to sit *between* the two trees, so the rear one makes a leaning place and the front one conceals him and supports the rifle. It isn't always possible to find such a setup, but it's worth searching for, even if it puts you farther from the squirrel tree you're watching.

One suggestion regarding the rifle support. Don't place the gun itself against the tree. Rather, grip the fore-end normally with the forward hand and contrive a way of solidly supporting the hand against the tree. Often you can find the stub of a

The best squirrel stand is one between two trees, so you are concealed, have a place to rest your back and a support for the rifle. But sometimes you take what you can get and make the most of it, as here. (Photo by P.J. Bell.)

A natural rest such as this tree stub makes precise aiming—and therefore instant kills—easy for a squirrel hunter. It pays to find such an aid as soon as you take a stand. (Photo by P.J. Bell.)

57

limb or a crease in the bark to give a good purchase. This is not to protect the gun from scratches, but rather because guns touching a solid object sometimes "shoot away" from it. That is, if the right side of the fore-end is held solidly against the tree, the bullet's point of impact may be farther left than expected. The variation usually isn't much (and some guns have no noticeable change), but when your target can be smaller than a postage stamp, any variation can mean a miss. Experimental shooting before the season on targets at known distances can indicate how your rifle/ammo combination reacts to such handling.

Searching for Rimfire Accuracy

In line with that, it's highly advisable to try different makes and styles of ammunition in a gun. Almost always results will be decidedly superior with one make and anything from very good to lousy with the others. High-grade target ammo usually is the most accurate, even in hunting guns, and is well worth its extra price to serious squirrel shooters. However, today's high speed hollow point ammunition is far superior in accuracy to that available when I was a kid. Again, different makes and bullet styles will shoot differently in different guns—and even vary from lot to lot among the same make—but it's usually easy to find something that your gun will put into less than 1½ inches at 50 yards, and that will handle most squirrel shooting. Target ammo from a target rifle, or a few top-quality sporters, will often put 10 shots in less than ½-inch at that distance, but comparatively few hunters want to carry the heavy outfits or pay for the expensive ones. Hollow point bullets are more destructive on squirrels than solids or target ammo, but this isn't necessary if placement is good. I pick the load that will give the best groups and then try to place my shot precisely where it will do the most good.

I did try a target outfit, incidentally. Somewhere along the way I decided that if the little M72 and 29-S did a good job, the bull barrel M52 Winchester and 18X Unertl 1½-inch target scope I'd acquired for competitive shooting ought to be even more effective. It didn't work out that way. From the shooting bench, the 52 would just chew ragged-hole groups at 50 yards—less than half the size of the little hunting gun's—but the high magnification scope drove me crazy in the woods. It was rarely in focus, as shots came at any range from 10 to 70 yards, the field was too small to quickly find my target, and everything looked so different when magnified that much that it was just impractical. And of course the outfit weighed too much for any sensible person to lug. I killed a few squirrels with it, but none that I'd have missed with the old M72, so I gave up quickly on that experiment.

Reduced Centerfire Loads

I kept trying other rifles, through the years. Some guys are like that. Most of them were conventional hunting outfits, like the M61 Winchester slide action, but a few deserve mention if only to show how nutty a hunter can be. I've mentioned wanting a .218 Bee for chucks. Somewhere along the way, I got one on a swap—a M65 Winchester lever action with Weaver 440 scope in a Stith Streamline mount, as cute a little quick-shooter as ever came down the pike. It didn't have blinding accuracy, but it wasn't bad, and one fall I decided to brew up some reduced loads and use it as my squirrel rifle for the year. I did, and it worked reasonably well if I made head shots. I mean, the head wasn't there anymore and the shoulders were somewhat bloodshot, but the squirrel died. I even made a few shots on running squirrels, which is no mean feat, if you'll excuse my immodesty. Trouble was, I didn't hit these in the head, so there wasn't a lot left. I concluded even my reduced loads were a bit much—they probably still equaled the factory Hornet—and decided to forget the Bee for squirrel

shooting and keep it for chucks. I soon outgrew it there, of course—its range was just too limited.

The Bee was followed in short order by a number of high velocity varmint rifles, including several .219 Donaldson Wasps, a couple of .22-250s and a .222 Sako. These of course were primarily woodchuck and crow outfits, but several of them were drafted for squirrel shooting at various times. My first Wasp gave me one of my more interesting squirrel shooting experiences. While crow hunting one fall day, I happened to spot a big gray high in a walnut tree. The season was open so I decided to take him. With a 50-gr. bullet loaded to some 3400 fps, I knew a shoulder shot would destroy everything, so decided to go for the head. It would have been a long shot for a rimfire, 90 yards or so, but that was easy pickings with the Wasp and its 10x Edwards scope, and I wasn't surprised when the squirrel tumbled. I walked over and found it beneath the tree, lying on its back, head away from me. I happened to pick it up with my left hand, first two fingers around its throat, thumb and other fingers grasping the body beneath the front legs. It was fortunate I had that kind of grip, for when I touched that old bushytail it was like turning on the switch of a buzzsaw. He couldn't get loose—my hand automatically clamped down when I felt him surge—but in a manner of speaking neither could I. And I'd have liked to! His teeth and front claws couldn't get at me, but there was nothing between his hind claws and my wrist but brisk autumn air. He really did rake me over before I somehow ended the incident. To this day, I don't know how I finally killed him. When it was all over, I found that my bullet had cut a narrow groove in the top of his head, knocking him out just long enough for me to walk over and pick him up. I don't know if a rimfire bullet would have the same effect as that from the high-speed Wasp—I've never duplicated that shot—but ever since then I've made it a practice to be certain that any animal I shoot is dead before I pick it up or try to do anything at all with it. You're supposed to learn from experience, I've been told, and I sure learned something from that incident.

A season or so later, I decided to try for a turkey gobbler with a rifle, and picked a favorite .22-250 for the chore. It was built on a double-set-trigger M98 Mauser action with a premium grade Pfeiffer barrel, topped with a 6x Zeiss Zielsechs scope in which T.K. Lee had installed one of his famous Floating Dot reticles. It seemed likely that full power loads wouldn't leave anything edible if I connected with the eating meat, so I brewed up some reduced loads using the 45-gr. Hornet bullet at a velocity of about 2200 fps. This turned out to be an extremely accurate combination, and one early winter day I took it on a squirrel hunt. As often happens in central Pennsylvania at that time of year, the weather turned miserable: rain and sleet that froze on top of 4 inches of old snow. I didn't think any squirrel would be out in that stuff, and was tempted to call it quits before getting out of the car. But I didn't (it seems I never do), and before long I was working through a stand of big hemlocks which gave a little protection against the weather. I'd gone only a couple of hundred yards when I spotted a gray sitting in the crotch of a tree, huddled against the trunk, big tail protecting its back, eyes closed, apparently sleeping. I watched it for quite awhile, puzzled as to why a critter that could be curled up in a snug den somewhere would choose to ignore the elements and do its snoozing out in the open. But I suppose it could have wondered much the same thing about me, had it known I was there. It never learned that. I eased over against the trunk of another hemlock, quietly set the Mauser's trigger, put the Lee Dot on the base of the squirrel's head and touched the front trigger. There was a *splatt*, and the silver-gray critter dropped to the ground, four legs and tail extended by reflex action, decapitated.

For several hours I saw nothing else, and I was making my way back to the car when I spotted another big gray moving in the top of a dark hemlock. There was no opportunity to find a rest for the gun, and I prepared for an offhand shot if one should be presented. But though I could see occasional movement in the tree, I never got a clear view of the squirrel. Eventually it vanished completely, and I stood there with the gun half raised, hoping it would reappear. It did—going straight down the trunk of the hemlock. Its entire body was exposed, the back toward me, but I didn't think there was the slightest chance I could hit it. Connecting on a moving squirrel with a rifle is a sometimes thing under the best of circumstances, and swinging downward is an unnatural thing that in no way qualifies for ''best'' rating. Nevertheless, I flipped up the gun, somehow managed to get the critter in the scope, dipped the muzzle down and touched the trigger. The bullet centered the spine for an instant kill.

They were the only shots I had that day, but besides proving the efficiency of that load—it killed well without the destructiveness of the Bee loads I'd been using—it showed it pays to get into the woods every chance you have, even if the weather seems impossible. Most small game animals will not be out in miserable conditions, of course, but there are exceptions to the rule, and they can make a day you'll remember for years. And any day spent hunting, whether you bag anything or not, is better than a day spent in near stupor in front of the TV set.

Somewhere along the way I reasoned that if reduced loads in the .22-250 worked okay on squirrels, it should be even easier to get something suitable in the smaller-capacity .222. I again chose the 45-gr. Hornet bullet for experimentation, this time the Sierra round nose. It seemed probable these lightly constructed bullets would expand better at the lower velocities than the 50- or 55-gr. spitzers designed for 3500 fps or more; also, since I used spitzers exclusively for varmint shooting, it was easy to visually recognize the different loads if necessary.

I had a good supply of fast-burning Unique powder, which seemed a reasonable choice in the .222. Almost no testing was required to come up with a suitable combination. I started with 4 grs., went to 4½ and 5, loading 10 rounds of each, half of each combination using one-eighth sheet of toilet tissue crumpled up and tamped in on top of the powder to hold it in place against the primer. So far as accuracy in the Sako went, all were suitable. At 50 yards, benchrest, when there was no wind to outguess, all three loads tended to pile the bullets up in one hole. Even with an occasional wide shot, groups measured under ¾-inch, which meant they would hit squirrels in the head at that distance. At various times I checked the velocity of the 5-gr. load on an Avtron K-233 and an Oehler chronograph, and it averaged 1735 fps. This is about midway between high speed Long Rifle rimfire ammo and the reduced load I'd been using in the .22-250, and a good number of grays taken with it showed excellent killing power without extreme destructiveness.

With a 6x Lyman All-American scope on the Sako, that load was my favorite on squirrels for a number of years. I had no complaints at all, yet somewhere below the surface I suppose there was always the nagging realization that squirrels really were supposed to be shot with .22 rimfire. (There's little rational argument for such a feeling . . . anything that does the job well should be acceptable . . . yet there it was, probably the result of decades of subtle brainwashing by various friends and magazine articles.)

Rimfires Are for Squirrels

One day while talking with gunsmith Al Wardrop, we got onto the subject of his old 52 Winchester, a standard-weight,

Squirrel hunters spend a lot of time looking upward, as Don Lewis is doing here, 'cause that's the direction they usually see their game and shoot. Don's outfit is a M64 Savage/Anschutz with 6x Unertl target scope. At 60 yards the odds are good it'll put its first shot in the ear orifice of an old gray. Though a bit bulky and heavy, its accuracy is phenomenal.

speedlock target model built in the mid-'30s. He'd used it for years of competitive shooting, including a period just after World War II when we shot on opposing teams in a small league, but both of us had given up such shooting long ago. The upshot of the conversation was a swap that gave me the 52.

I figured that if I were going to have a 52 Winchester as a squirrel rifle, it should be as close to my ideal gun as I could make it. So I had Al cut the barrel to 21 inches, recess crown it, and alter and install a Conetrol scope base so a scope would sit just forward of the bolt handle. While that was being done, I ordered a Mannlicher-style tigertail maple stock blank from Bishop, along with a Niedner-type steel buttplate and grip cap. I'm no stockmaker, but I wanted to do this job myself, and after some weeks of spare time work I finished inletting, shaping and suigi-finishing the stock. Because fore-ends of

The author with an adult gray taken in winter season. Weather can be miserable at this time of year, but the hunting is good.

mention specific results with different makes of ammo because they wouldn't necessarily be pertinent. The kind that gave the worst results in my gun could give the best results in yours, or vice versa. It doesn't matter in the slightest what ammo your hunting buddy uses, or even where your personal preferences might be. The final choice should be determined by what your rifle likes, and it takes serious testing to determine this.

After making the selection, it's a pious idea to shoot it at 10-yard intervals out to 50 or 60 yards, so you can see precisely where your impact will be in relation to your aiming point. A squirrel's body is long and narrow, which means there is little room for vertical error when shooting at one stretched out on a limb. Exact scope zeroing and familiarity with the bullet's trajectory are therefore important. In one test with the M52 after zeroing in at 50 yards, I fired three shots from 10, 20, 30, 40 and 50 yards. Thirteen of the 15 shots went into a ragged hole measuring about ³/₁₆-inch wide and well under an inch vertically; the two "wild" shots bracketed the group, making its overall width about an inch. Every shot would have hit a squirrel's head, but it's worth knowing that the three fired from 10 yards were the bottom ones in the group and those from 20 yards were still a whisper under exact zero. The nine shots from 30, 40 and 50 yards went into about ⅜-inch. The height of the scope's optical center above the boreline makes it possible to utilize a long arc of the bullets' trajectory this way, in effect giving a point blank range from 10 to 50 yards. Three shots fired at 60 yards measured ⅝-inch and were about an inch below the center of impact of the other 15, enough to cause a miss if no allowance were made for drop. This illustrates the importance of knowing the range precisely, once it gets beyond 50 yards.

The M52 has become my favorite squirrel rifle. It's a bit heavy, but that's no problem in the easy-to-navigate eastern woods; in fact, it makes for steady holding. The first squirrel of the past season was typical of most of those taken with it. Again, it was a wet mid-October day, the woods gloomy and dripping in the afternoon even after the rain stopped. I was leaning against a small oak, wishing I hadn't forgotten my binoculars, when I saw a cutting drift down from the upper branches of another oak. A moment's searching with the

Mannlicher stocks have a tendency to warp, I chiseled out a groove as wide and deep as possible from just ahead of the action to near the front end and filled it with glass bedding. I discarded the pressed-steel trigger guard assembly, installed an anodized aluminum one from the M700 ADL Remington, and filed out and fitted a metal plate to enclose the bottom of the clip. Quick detachable swivels and a braided leather carrying sling completed the job.

While all this was going on, I sent a 6x Leupold Golden Ring scope to the T.K. Lee Co. and had a pair of dots installed, a 2 minute-of-angle dot at the cross hair intersection and a 1 minute dot 6 minutes beneath. The larger dot subtends just 1-inch at 50 yards, which is close to the eye-to-eye measurement of an adult gray squirrel facing the gun, or the eye-to-ear measurement on a side view. The dot thus serves as a good rangefinder up to distances where it blots out the head. At longer ranges, the 6-MOA separation of the two dots is helpful in the same way, and the lower dot can be used for precise aiming out around the 100-yard mark, the exact zero depending upon the ammo being used. Only test firing will give this information precisely, but this is easily carried out.

I got so much satisfaction out of this remodeled 52 that I spent many evenings at the bench, testing as many kinds of Long Rifle ammunition as I could find. A couple of thousand shots were fired in a short period, most shooting being done in the calm just before dusk. Some 5-shot groups went into aspirin-size holes, while others measured over an inch. I don't

Though the author prefers a scoped rifle for squirrels, a shotgun is best under some conditions, and also will handle grouse.

Good binoculars add greatly to a hunter's efficiency, making it easy to tell if a suspicious bump on a limb is a squirrel or a knot. Full-size glasses of 6x30, 7x35 or 8x40 are superior to the compact designs as they transmit more light in dark woods where these critters live. (Photo by P.J. Bell.)

scope revealed a squirrel industriously searching for more mast to cut. The foliage concealed most of him, making a precise shot impossible, but it was possible to keep him in the scope's field as he moved through the upper reaches of the tree. Then he went out of sight, but I'd noted his direction was downward and was soon lucky enough to spot him descending one of the larger limbs. I tracked him with the Lee Dc waiting for him to stop. When he did, his head was behind a branch and leaves concealed his entire body except for the neck. But I'd seen him stop and knew I was looking at a vital area, so placed the dot on it and gently squeezed the trigger. The *splat* drifted through the wet woods, and I saw my target come cartwheeling down to thump solidly in the soaked oak leaves that blanketed the ground. The hollow point Super-X bullet had broken the neck for an instant kill. Another wet weather hunt had paid off.

Despite my fondness for the M52, when I recently had a chance to acquire a M581 Remington at a good price, I couldn't pass it up. This is a lightweight clip-fed, bolt action sporter. It has a decent trigger and the action is grooved for tip-off mounts. They aren't my favorites for mounting a scope on a rifle, but I got a pair, installed a 4x Lyman All-American scope with a 2-MOA Lee Dot reticle, and traipsed out to the range. From the bench, with ammo it liked, this little Remington often put five shots into ½-inch at 50 yards. This is more accuracy than most squirrel shooters actually need, and it comes in a package that's easily carried all day and can be obtained by simply walking into a sporting goods store and paying a reasonable amount of money. Such a happening can give pause to a feller who thinks he has to go to crazy extremes to get an outfit to shoot something. (Which gives some insight into the derivation of the term "gun-nut," I suppose.)

Scopes

It should be noted that all the scopes I've used for squirrels except for the first little 29-S Weaver have been models normally thought of as big game designs. There's good reason for this. Since just after World War II, almost all such scopes have been built on 1-inch tubes, with enlarged objectives if over 3x and have had lenses coated with magnesium fluoride. These characteristics have greatly increased light transmission, compared to the ¾-inch tubes typical of scopes designed for use on .22 rimfires. This is highly important in the dark woods where most squirrel sniping is done. Adjustments also tend to be more accurate than those of the inexpensive models. Doubtless it's cost that keeps more hunters from using the big game models on squirrels, but when you consider how much shooting bushytails can give compared with deer, say, it makes sense to go with the best. As to magnification, 2½x will do for most chances, with 6x plenty for the longest ranges a .22 rimfire can handle. A good all around choice is 4x, with medium-weight crosswires or 2-MOA center dot reticle; the latter subtends 1-inch at 50 yards, so its advantages are obvious.

Bullet Placement

Despite the fact that I've mentioned a number of head shots, that's not my favorite aiming point on squirrels. Many hunters prefer it, and it's obviously deadly when the brain is hit. However, if the rifle is not precisely zeroed in, or there's a slight error on the shooter's part, the bullet can easily hit the nose or jaw area instead of the brain, and you then have a badly wounded animal escaping through the treetops to die a lingering death of starvation or infection. No sportsman wants this. So I prefer to drive my bullets through the shoulders or lungs, the same kind of placement commonly advised for big game killing with centerfire loads. The reasoning is the same: These are vital areas which when struck by a bullet of appropriate size are quickly fatal. The shoulder shot puts a squirrel out of action at once if the bones are hit. He simply cannot get away if his front quarters are smashed. This placement causes some bloodshot meat, but overnight soaking in cold salt water usually takes care of that. As with big game, a slightly high shot will break the spine for an instant kill, while forward placement might catch the neck and a bullet slightly to the rear will still hit the lungs. This might not kill instantly, but a lung-shot squirrel rarely goes far. What it all boils down to is this: The shoulder-lung aiming point is the largest vital area, and even if your bullet placement is ½-inch off it will still kill, whereas that much error on a head shot can allow the squirrel to run off and slowly starve to death. If you do prefer the head shot, or circumstances offer nothing else, favor the rear portion as your aiming point when taking a shot from the side. Stay away from the jaws.

When, Where and How to Bag Bushytails

Early morning and late afternoon are usually the best times to be in the squirrel woods, especially when after grays. More of the critters are out and about at these times, doing what wild animals spend a great deal of their time doing—eating. Sometimes you can't get there too early. Late last season I happened to be in a good oak-grown ravine long before daylight, and there were squirrels everywhere. Moving, feeding, just running around, barely visible even when they passed close to me. I don't know how many I saw or heard in the dry leaves, but I never got a shot. It was too dark to aim even with the top-quality Leupold scope, and when the light strengthened enough that I could have shot, they were gone. And they didn't reappear during the long hours I spent there. These were grays. Fox squirrels don't usually get moving so early.

Nevertheless, to bag squirrels you have to get into squirrel country at the right time, so you play the odds and emphasize the morning and evening times. Picking the right area isn't always easy. Scouting is greatly helpful, but few hunters will actually go out ahead of the open season. They scout and hunt simultaneously, if that makes sense. Basically, most efforts should be spent somewhat within the edges of woods that have mast-producing trees such as hickories and white oaks, plus some good denning trees. If there's still some standing corn in nearby fields, that helps. In late fall I've seen squirrels come out of such fields in what seemed to be hordes when a pheasant hunter kicked through. Corn is not always a favorite food, yet at times they do hit it hard. Wooded ravines or "waste" areas overgrown with grapevines often intrude between crop fields, and these provide more chances at squirrels than most hunters realize. Squirrels don't necessarily live in these little spots—that is, they might sleep elsewhere—but they loaf here, or carry ears of corn into such cover to eat, or just fool around in the tangles, out of the wind and basking in the sun when the mood strikes them. Any pockets of food will attract squirrels, especially late in the season.

You can't expect much shooting by simply going out in an untested area and sitting down to wait for squirrels to come to you. Go to them, moving slowly and as quietly as possible, watching and listening for movement in the trees and on the ground. Squirrels spend a big percentage of their time on the ground where undisturbed, so don't look upward constantly. When you do find game, ease into range, even if your approach sends them in. Find a position that will let you cover the area, with a convenient rest for your rifle. Don't sit with the sun in your eyes. Then wait—silently and motionlessly. Any movement now should be at the approximate speed of a glacier. If you must move a hand or arm, try to keep it within the outline of your body so it doesn't get silhouetted. If you hear something in the leaves outside your field of view, try to see it by moving the eyes only; move the head only if absolutely necessary . . . and then so slowly you can hardly stand it. The hunter's face is one of the most visible things in the woods. It shines like a beacon in a wild animal's view. So it's advisable to skip shaving before heading to the woods. A billed cap or brimmed hat that casts a shadow over the face also is helpful. Clothes should have a soft finish for quiet movement and be neutral colored to blend into the background. If other hunters normally frequent the same woods, a bit of fluorescent orange is a good safety factor. Sewed to the back of your shoulders and hat, it won't be seen by squirrels in front of you, yet will stand out for hunters to your rear. Squirrels aren't much bothered by colors anyway, so long as movement is slow.

Binoculars are a tremendous help in locating game. Their light-gathering quality and magnification often make it possible to determine if a suspicious bump on a distant limb is just a knot or a squirrel's head. They're far superior to the rifle scope for searching, though the scope is useful for examining something you've chanced to see with the naked eye but can't identify. As there's always a chance that what you'll be looking at will turn out to be another hunter, anytime you use the scope this way make it an absolute rule to open the rifle's action first. That way it will be impossible for the gun to fire. If the object is game, it takes only a moment to close the bolt and prepare to shoot.

I prefer full size binoculars for squirrel hunting. They are heavier and bulkier than the compacts, but the latter are usually about 6x21 or 8x21 in size, which means their exit pupils will be only around 3 millimeters in diameter, which gives poor light transmission. A 7x35, will have a 5 millimeter exit pupil, and a 7x50 will have a 7 millimeter pupil, and these are far superior when ambient light is poor. Lens quality can be as high in the compacts as in any, if you buy the quality makes, and this will give good resolution when light is good, but in dark woods you need the bigger lenses for serious searching.

So get a good pair of binoculars and a good scope-sighted rifle, and get yourself into the squirrel woods this fall. You'll find that bushwacking bushytails is one of the most challenging hunting games going.

CHAPTER 8
Ringnecked Pheasant

I MIGHT AS WELL ADMIT it here and now: The ringneck pheasant is my favorite upland bird. I'll hunt anything that's in season, every chance I get for as long as shooting light holds, and enjoy every minute of it; yet if circumstances somehow forced me to choose just one game bird to chase for the rest of my shooting life, the choice would be easy. I'd pick the bold, brash, gaudy, loudmouthed, longtailed import from China, the ringneck.

The choice wouldn't even be difficult. Just consider the possible alternatives.

The ruffed grouse could well be the popular choice if a referendum were taken of hunters, but I often wonder why since most of them never hunt this bird. Admittedly, the grouse is a lovely bird, a difficult and demanding target under ordinary circumstances. At least that's the way it's portrayed in all the outdoor magazines and bird-hunting books which have influenced so many readers. But you've got to remember that these stories are crafted by individuals who love this dignified brown bird, and their writings can't help but reflect their personal feelings. What they almost never mention is that it takes a peculiar set of circumstances to make the grouse the great game bird they describe. When grouse are plentiful and largely unhunted, as in parts of southeastern Canada in recent years, for instance, they are not great game birds at all.

Jim Bashline is going into action as Sam busts a nice rooster out of some thick weeds, reacting quicker to the flush than Harry Plitt.

Jim Bashline and Don Lewis compare the pheasants they bagged one morning. Mixed ancestry of American pheasants is sometimes reflected in their feather coloration.

average, and these shots are the kind to challenge a good shotgunner's ability, and the bird bagged is impressive in itself, for the amount and quality of its flesh as well as for the difficulty in bagging it, can a given species be named the top game bird. When conditions are ideal—enough but not too many birds—the grouse certainly qualifies for this position. However, due to its cyclic population, conditions are not ideal about 70 percent of the time.

So what does that leave us? Doves? They're usually plentiful, can be difficult to hit until you get the hang of it, and are certainly good eating. But so far as hunting goes, they're undemanding. Woodcock? They're too comical to take seriously. Quail? The shooting is fun and the eating is delicious, but the dogs do most of the hunting, and too many quail hunts are really social affairs. Turkey? An old gobbler is really big game. So what does that leave us? Ringnecks. The ringneck is famous for being an import that made good. I don't know why that should be unusual in this country, where almost all of us are descendants of immigrants who arrived within the last couple of hundred years and a certain percentage do succeed, but it seems to stick in the minds of sportsmen.

The ringneck is an Asiatic bird. It's often thought of as having Chinese ancestry, probably because the first successful stocking in this country was of birds from the Shanghai region, and some older hunters still call them "Chinks." However, more than 40 subspecies of pheasants are found in Asia, and some of those used in various stocking endeavors in the United States came, if indirectly, from the region between the Black and Caspian seas, some 5000 miles west of Shanghai, while still others came from east of China, the Japanese islands. The pheasant is thus seen to be native to a vast stretch of Asia, from some 50 degrees north latitude to 10 degrees south, and from about 40 degrees to 145 degrees east longitude. Furthermore, one subspecies or another has been found at all altitudes from sea level to over 16,000 feet in the

The day was wet and foggy, but any day after roosters is a good one, and a few hours brought a pair of birds for both Chuck Fergus and the author.

They seem almost tame, they fly with reluctance. Admittedly, once airborne in the tangles they inhabit there, they are difficult to hit, but there's something unnatural about watching them parade around on the ground, ignoring you until you are close enough to almost grab them with your bare hands.

I've seen essentially the same thing while elk hunting in the Pacific Northwest. We occasionally came onto a half-dozen or so sitting in a tree, and again they exhibited a strong reluctance to fly. Bob Balbach sometimes killed enough with stones to make our supper, and occasional Idaho hunters I knew carried slingshots for the same chore. Harry Stubblefield packed a Hi-Standard .22 auto pistol for the same purpose and shot hundreds over the years, and I once watched Andy Hufnagle knock the heads off five with his .243, from about 70 yards, starting with the bottom one and working up, as the old-time hunters always recommended. I've often thought that the big bags market hunters made in years gone by—400 to 500 in a few months by some part-time hunters in central Pennsylvania, for instance—were helped along by the comparative tameness of grouse under certain conditions. To say that this kind of shooting is a sporting challenge has to bring raised eyebrows.

Conversely, when populations are so low that a hunter can tramp from dawn till dark, along rough wooded ridges and through thick tangled swamps, and scarcely hear a flush let alone get a shot, it's pointless to insist that the grouse is our greatest upland game bird. Only when the situation is such that a hard day's hunt will produce a couple of shots on the

Pheasants like messes such as this, particularly if they're near feeding areas. Most ringneck hunters work them out automatically, or send the dog in.

Himalayas. That takes in a good chunk of real estate in anyone's language, though of course there are large areas within those boundaries where pheasants are not found.

Though a jungle fowl, pheasants have long been familiar to man, and over 3000 years ago Chinese artisans embroidered their likenesses on silk tapestries. Five hundred years before the birth of Christ, the Greeks saw these birds along the Phasis River in the Colchis area between the Black and Caspian seas. Later, the Romans gained control of much of this region, and they named this longtailed bird *Phasianus avis,* or "the bird from the Phasis." During the expansion of the Roman Empire, this bird was "stocked" in Europe and Britain, where it became one of the ancestors of the English "blackneck" pheasant. The name *Phasianus* became *fagiano* in Italian, *faisan* in French, *Fasan* in German, and *pheasant* in English.

English pheasants were used in the first known stocking attempt in North America. This took place about 1730, when Colonel John Montgomery, governor of the colony of New York, released a few birds on Nutten Island. All shortly vanished. Some 60 years later, Richard Bache, son-in-law of Ben Franklin, also put out some English pheasants, without success. Various other attempts at stocking this bird were tried, but not until 1881 were there any positive results. That year, Judge O.H. Denny, U.S. Consul General at Shanghai, succeeded in delivering several dozen pheasants to the farm of his brother near Corvallis in Oregon's Willamette Valley. The environment suited them and they thrived, and before many years had passed their descendants were providing shooting for countless hunters in many parts of this country.

Not all of our pheasants are a result of that first Oregon stocking, of course. Through the years that followed, numerous imports were made from different areas of Asia and Europe, and it seems fair to say that the American pheasant, if we can call it that, is the offspring of four subspecies. The bird supplied by Judge Denny doubtless was *Phasianus colchicus torquatus,* a native of eastern and southeastern China. It is

notable for the white collar or neck ring, which usually is interrupted in front. *Phasianus colchicus colchicus,* the pheasant of Transcaucasia, is the one native to the Black and Caspian seas region which the Romans and others spread over much of Europe and Britain. *Phasianus colchicus mongolicus,* the Mongolian pheasant, and the *Phasianus versicolor,* the green pheasant of Japan, made up the bulk of the remaining stockings. These subspecies, which vary somewhat in coloration, interbreed freely, and it is not unusual to bag pheasants anywhere from the Pacific Northwest to the Atlantic seaboard that reflect their mixed heritage. In general, though, most of the American males look pretty much alike, a coppery-red with black markings on the body, dark belly, often greenish-gray rump feathers, near-black iridescent tufted head with scarlet cheek patches, and the snow-white collar that gives him his common name of "ringneck." And of course the splendid tail whose longest feathers sometimes exceed 2 feet in length. He's a striking looking critter.

The females are far from resplendent, being mainly a drab brown or tan with black markings above, buff color below. But just because they're unspectacular in appearance doesn't mean they're unimportant. They're what makes it possible for hunters in all parts of this country except the Southeast and Southwest to get some of their best days afield. As John Madson once put it, this is the bird that laid the golden egg. Though the pheasant is easy to breed on game farms for release ahead of the hunting season, it's still the wild birds, the survivors of long-gone stockings which fought their way through sometimes adverse conditions to produce at least one more generation on their own, that supply most of the pheasant hunting in America. In total, the birds from these hunts have added up to hundreds of millions of main courses on gunners' tables. Not bad for a species which has been in this country for less than a century. Even that makes me wonder why we should still think of the pheasant as an import here. After all, did your ancestors live here for almost a hundred generations?

much of the time—a habit which has not endeared him to hunters, especially those who like to use pointing dogs.

Breeding and Habitat

The sexes tend to separate during the winter, but in early spring the roosters begin to feel the sex urge. Mature birds select a territory and begin crowing. This attracts females, or at least lets them know that something is going on, and notifies other cockbirds that this area has been claimed. A battle can result if another rooster moves into the area. When a hen shows some interest in his crowing, the rooster entices her closer with a quiet clucking sound, sometimes offers her bits of food and then goes into his Big Act—a proud strut that is really something to see, be you a little ol' hen or binocular-packing voyeur. With his neck feathers fluffed and head low, the rooster advances on the hen. The wing nearest her is extended downward, feathers flared, and his long tail is extended and displayed. His ear tufts are erect, his cheek patches a flaming scarlet. He struts back and forth, constantly presenting his impressive colors for her admiration. The hen shows little emotion about all these goings-on, but eventually the rooster collects a number of willing partners and they get on with perpetuating the species.

Pheasant nests are casual affairs built by the hen. A few dry weeds compressed in a slight depression in a hayfield make up the typical nest, though one might be found most anywhere—in fencerows, weedy ditches, whatever. Early on, several hens may deposit a number of eggs in the same "dump nest" before getting down to productive business. The usual clutch is six to 12 eggs, the larger number being typical earlier in the season. The hen does the incubating, which takes about 23 days. Fertility is good, usually over 85 percent, but because ground nests are easy pickings for many predators—skunks, opossums, 'coons, snakes, crows—and are susceptible to fires, high water and mowing, many eggs and chicks are destroyed. If this occurs, many hens re-nest and try again, and occasionally hens try even a third time. Clutches are hatched as early as May and as late as September, but most chicks are out by July.

Chicks weigh less than an ounce and are precocial, though the hen shields them against inclement weather for several weeks. Most of their early diet consists of insects, which are high in protein. In 2 weeks they can fly short distances. Adult plumage begins to show at 4 to 6 weeks and is complete at 5 months. Adult birds eat almost any plant that grows where they live—corn, barley, wheat, oats, sorghum, rice, fruit, seeds of many kinds, smartweed, chickweed, berries, kale, sumac, whatever—plus insects of most kinds up to mouse size. They're more interested in quantity than quality, though when conditions get bad they can survive for weeks with almost no food at all.

According to a few million experienced hunters, pheasants are where you find 'em. The touch of alliteration probably makes that an easily remembered aphorism, but it has the further quality of truth. Anyone who has spent more than one full season hunting ringnecks knows that any type of cover that exists in a pheasant area is going to be utilized by these longtailed spooks. Traditionally, corn country is pheasant country, and it's true that they are found in such fields, both big and small. We've kicked them out of a tiny sweet corn patch in the backyard, getting properly cussed out for our intrusion as they left; and, in cooperation with platoon-size groups of shotgun toters, have flushed hordes of them from Midwestern cornfields that stretched horizon to horizon. But cornfields aren't the only place they're found. In fact, since most of today's farmers don't want hunters and their dogs clumping end to end in their standing corn, such areas are yielding fewer birds now than formerly. (The restriction is

This is the kind of place ringnecks sneak into when they hear guns banging. It's not easy to get through such tangles, let alone to put birds out of them, but pheasant hunters become used to such challenges because this is where the roosters are. Tough canvas and leather clothes are recommended.

Pheasants belong to the Phasianidae family, which is part of the order Galliformes, thus are described as gallinaceous, which means they scratch for a living. Among the ground cover, that is, for seeds, bugs, grubs, whatever. A lot of other birds which might appear unrelated also belong to this order, including quail, grouse, turkeys, prairie chickens and ptarmigan. Here, we're interested only in the ringneck.

Besides being far more colorful than the female, called a hen, the male or rooster is considerably larger. A young adult weighs about 2½ pounds, an older one perhaps 3½, and a fat old-timer as much as 4 pounds. Bub Mausteller of Danville, Pennsylvania has told me that in the mid-'30s he weighed a central-Pennsylvania rooster that went just over 5 pounds. I never saw one that weighed anywhere near that much, but I think it's possible for an occasional individual of any species to get bigger than average. By comparison, an average hen weighs about 2 pounds.

Both sexes have pointed tails, the male's being especially long and impressive, short rounded wings, and powerful rangy legs. The ratio of wing area to body weight is poor, which makes for a fairly rapid wingbeat and reasonably fast but not long flight. Perhaps it's the pheasant's leg/wing characteristics which make him prefer running to flying so

(Above) Circling, quartering, reverse-angling—such maneuvers are often necessary if a lone hunter is to boot ringnecks out of cover like this. If the hunter just runs through in a straight path, shrewd old cockbirds will simply move aside and squat, leaving him with only sore and tired legs to show for his time afield.

(Right) Small grass clumps like this provide plenty of conceal-ment for ringnecks and should be kicked out thoroughly. Flushed birds are easy pickings here.

(Below) When a rooster takes off close in a field like this, he's in trouble if the hunter remembers to concentrate on his head and ignore his tail. Chuck Fergus hit the right end for a clean kill—not always easy on this big tough critter.

basically a matter of economics: too many hunters carelessly knock down standing corn, making it difficult to pick mechan-ically, thus costing the landowner money.)

Pheasants can vanish on a putting green, so any kind of natural cover is more than enough to conceal them. Hip-high weedfields often contain ringnecks, as do overgrown fence-rows, sumac- and bramble-grown ravines and farm dumps (make sure your tetanus immunization is up to date before clumping around in these rusty-can ditches), thickly grown patches and corners near crop fields or the past summers vegetable gardens, sidehills of autumn olive, forgotten cor-ners where several different-type fields touch a creek, skinny weedy strips between fields of winter wheat, cattail marshes where cover is thick late in the season, small woodlots partly or wholly surrounded by more typical pheasant cover, tiny openings—as where a big tree has fallen—in larger tracts of woods if there is enough pressure in fields within ¼-mile or so to move birds into the trees, thick stretches of cover

Tangled corners like this often conceal ringnecks. The hunter can kick them out himself, if he's in good physical condition and the day isn't too long, but a dog makes things easier. He not only finds and flushes game, he also brings it back.

along creekbanks, steep overgrown banks paralleling railroad tracks. These are the sorts of places where roosters will be found.

Admittedly, this is at odds with the normal idea of pheasant cover. These big red birds are commonly seen strutting around the back forty in broad daylight, ambling out of the corn and across the winter wheat. Or along the edges of secondary roads, where they sometimes have to almost be forced out of your car's path. You may also see them sitting in a row on a sunny morning, six or eight of them, on a line of fenceposts, drying their gaudy feathers after enduring a night of solid rains. Witnessing such actions, hunters of little experience think that the only thing necessary for bagging a couple of these boobies on opening morning is a stroll out back of the barn and a couple of shells. Well, that can be true . . . on opening morning. After all, pheasants are farm country birds. They're used to people. They should be; they lived in proximity to countless hordes in China and Korea and elsewhere for thousands of years, and in their view there's no big difference between an Oriental and a South Dakota farmer. If you look at things from the birds' viewpoint, they probably think all those cornfields were planted for their exclusive use, and any humans are simply visitors or intruders. So the first few roosters in a season can be easy pickings. But that situation doesn't last. After the Big Bang—opening hour—things tend to quiet down in a hurry. Not because all the birds are dead. Most of them are still alive. But they've already realized that conditions have changed violently since sunrise, that they're up against a critter too big to trounce and probably too tough to eat if they had him on the ground, so they've done what any

survival expert would do under similar circumstances: "Squoze everything down into one little ball and vanished," as an old hunting buddy put it.

The hunter's job is to roust his quarry out of whatever cover it's in and kill it cleanly. The easy weedfields and cornfields, if permitted, are the places to hit when the season opens and the birds aren't yet alerted. How you'll handle them depends on various things, primarily whether you are alone or with friends, how many other hunters are in the area, if you have a dog and what kind, and so on.

Pheasant Dogs

Pheasants are not the favorite birds of those who admire good work by pointing dogs. The longtails simply don't play the game according to the same rules as quail or even woodcock or grouse. When a good pointer locks up in quail country, the gunner is practically certain there's something ahead of that quivering living statue, that when he moves in, something is going out, maybe just a rocketing single to test his skill, maybe 12 brown streaks that jar him as much as a machinegun burst. But what happens in pheasant country when he moves in behind his pointer or setter? Most of the time, nothing. Sure, there are occasions when a rooster is somewhere ahead of that straining nose, and booted out over an open field it can be an easy shot for a calm hunter, but most of the time there's nothing squatted in the weeds ahead of the dog. There was when he went on point, of course. But the pheasant never read the rules that say he's gotta stay there. Or if he did, he ignores them. "What is there about an ugly dog's snout that says I gotta sit and admire it?" he asks, and forthwith puts his long legs into motion and scuttles away, unseen, leaving utter frustration in his wake. It's common to have a dog lock up solid, then slowly soften, as if in disbelief, and almost reluctantly ease out of point and start to move ahead, following the scent of a critter he hasn't yet seen but which he knows has departed. This is such a common happening that many owners of good pointing breeds will not use them on pheasants for fear that they'll pick up bad habits.

This doesn't always happen, of course, and some hunters insist on using pointing dogs on ringnecks, and they get enough birds that they think they're enjoying it, so more power to 'em. But it does make an old unreconstructed pheasant-banger like me laugh when one of their wonders goes on point in the middle of a 300-acre field of standing corn, leaving them to wonder and whistle and eventually turn the air blue with their cussing.

Personally, we prefer flushing dogs for pheasants. A dog that will work close and nose into every bit of cover, circling and quartering to hit everything from every angle, will put out birds. And once that is done, the rest is up to the guy with the gun. Retrieving ability also is of great importance on pheasants, as it's easy to break a wing on a rooster and have it hit the ground running. So a dog with a good nose and a willingness to grab onto a 3-pound long-spurred scrambling bird can make the difference between getting and losing a good percentage of pheasants over a season. If buying a dog strictly for pheasants, it would come down to choosing between the springer spaniel and the Labrador retriever, for me. So far as pure hunting efficiency goes, at least before the shot is fired, the springer would probably take it. But a good Lab's retrieving ability is so great, and this is such a vital requirement on these tough birds, that it's easy to understand the constantly growing popularity of this breed in the uplands. The Lab's short hair doesn't require any after-hunt attention, either, and that can be a consideration following a full day in near-freezing rain and wet snow. So, you consider the advantages and disadvantages, make a choice and pay your money. And if you still want a pointer or setter, that's fine with me, too.

(Above) The grouse hunters get the wine-colored days. Pheasant bangers take what's left—such as this soggy one that John Behel, John Plowman and Jo are enduring.

(Left) A good dog always increases the hunter's efficiency and is especially helpful on ringnecks, which hit the ground running unless killed dead in the air—not always easy on these big tough birds. A dog's compansionship is also an asset.

(Below) The birds are in, so Sam (front and center) has other things on her mind. Howard Mortimer, the author, and Jim Bashline make like heroes with the roosters.

Weedfield pheasants often flush wild, but the author's M21 20-gauge is bored modified and full, and it handles chances like this well when he does his part.

Techniques for Taking Longtails

Because pheasants are such runners, it pays to use a hunting technique that blocks their escape routes. If three men are hunting together, one should be sent in a roundabout way to the far end of a fencerow or strip of standing corn that the other two will push out. The pheasant's mentality is such that he tends to either leave early, sometimes going out the far end of a fencerow almost as soon as you enter the other end, or he sits as tight as a stone, hanging in there with the nerve of a professional gambler as your number 10 boots clump down within inches of him and not stirring a millimeter. Interestingly, the gaudy coloration which makes him so conspicuous in the open provides near-perfect camouflage for a ringneck hiding in dense cover. Countless pheasants live to eat another day because the hunter naively thought that if he aimlessly wandered through the middle of a piece of cover, anything in it had to go out. Friend, that ain't so. Most pheasants take close contact—almost literal contact—to make them move. I have actually stepped on the tailfeathers of a cockbird hidden in a clump of grass smaller than a bed pillow, this in the middle of a pasture that couldn't conceal a white-footed mouse, before he flushed. And an occurrence like this, which is always unexpected even though you are stepping on such spots because you know a bird might be there, always takes you by surprise. As it happens, I killed this bird, but I've had them escape under similar circumstances.

So, you hit every bit of cover that you're passing, and sooner or later you'll get shooting on close-flushing birds. Your buddy who is blocking the far end will also get shooting at occasional early-leaving roosters. If you have no friend to do the blocking, you have to do it yourself. That might sound crazy, but it's not impossible. You do it by the way you hunt. If you simply wade through the weeds, making a beeline for the far end of the field so you can hit another one beyond, you're going to get little shooting. Pheasants are found in little places, near you, not in the next county. Look for 'em where you are instead of day-dreaming about how you'll bust 'em over yonder somewhere.

The pheasant's sense of sight and hearing are excellent, so if he understands that your course is going to take you safely past even if it's only a few feet to the side, he's just going to squat where he is and let you go on by. Or if he can move off to the side and squat again, he'll do that. The only way a lone hunter can overcome this is to move in an irregular pattern, changing direction often, moving in circles and squares or rectangles of different sizes, making certain to hit every clump of thick stuff at least once and preferably a couple of times from different directions. Silly? It might seem that way at first, and your friends might laugh a bit. But after you tally up the birds you've taken by repeated assaults on the same cover, you'll realize who's having the last laugh.

One important part of the circling and busting technique is standing still occasionally. This sounds contradictory, but it's based on knowing, or at least guessing, what the pheasant is thinking. Picture a tight corner of sumac, brambles and assorted brush. You feel certain a bird is hiding in there, and you've been clumping back and forth for what seems half a day, with no positive results. Then you pause for a breather, and after a minute that old rooster unexpectedly squawks his way upward through a couple layers of cover, scrambling into the air like a demented Spitfire pilot during the Battle of Britain. Why did he flush now, when nothing was happening, after playing hide and seek with you so long? Nobody knows for certain, but this is a common occurrence and it's probably a result of the rooster thinking you've quit moving because you're looking right at him. So with no other option available, he finally takes wing. And you kill him . . . maybe. A lot of times, this action is so unexpected that his bold move succeeds, and he arrows away into the distance, amber eyes

The author at the end of a day when things went better than normal. Sometimes the birds fly well and the gun points right and the kills are clean.

gleaming defiantly, raucous squawk hanging in the air like a personal insult, leaving you with an empty gun and a choice between laughing and cussing. After this has happened to you once or twice, you realize that a pause in the operations can be a deliberate thing on the hunter's part, and should be. So you pick the time and the place, making sure you halt where your feet are free of entangling creepers so you can move them quickly if necessary, and that your gun is ready and there's room to swing it. A broken-nerve rooster then becomes an easy target, and the result of a deliberate action on your part, which means you're a hunter, not just a lucky shooter.

Sometimes, of course, you can do everything right and still come out the loser. Or maybe both loser and winner in a philosophical sense. The past season provided an instance for me. Only a few miles from my home is a square of thick woods about 200 yards on a side. A blacktop road runs along one side and there's a pulloff at one corner where a car can be parked inside the woods. I left my Jeep there one afternoon and proceeded to thoroughly hunt that woods. I hit every bit of cover that seemed big enough to hide a mouse, but moved nothing. There was nothing to do but go elsewhere. When I was within 20 yards or so of the Jeep, I broke the SKB and pulled the loads out, thinking it just wasn't my day. Then I looked at the cover between me and the Jeep. A dozen steps' worth of raspberry brambles drifted with oak leaves. Just the sort of cover an old rooster would squat in, I thought, and wouldn't I feel silly if one went out and my gun was empty. So I reloaded the over-under, closed it, and took one step into the briars. And from right under my feet, out went a gaudy longtailed rooster, just as I'd anticipated, flying straight away, right smack over the top of my Jeep. I hadn't had an easier chance in years. It was made to order, a piece of cake, and it perfectly illustrated how a real pheasant hunter could outsmart even an old bird. This one was going to make a story I could brag a bit about. Such thoughts took only a moment, of

course, and by then I had flipped the gun to my shoulder and hit the trigger twice. Both shots were clean misses.

I just stared in literal amazement as that old cockbird went out of sight beyond a clear pasture on the other side of the road. I absolutely could not believe I'd missed him. But I had, as perfectly as if I'd practiced for months. My next inclination was to cuss, but I didn't do that either. It just wasn't appropriate. That great old bird had played his game to the limit, squatting there ahead of my Jeep while I parked and not moving an inch while I booted through the surrounding woods for half an afternoon, and still willing to let me walk by him and leave at the end. Then, when almost by accident I'd moved right onto him, with his life on the line he played his last ace and won. I just leaned against a tree and laughed. Friend, I'm telling you true, it wasn't only admiration for that old bird I felt, it was love. He's my kind of guy.

Sometimes it isn't appropriate to put out blockers, even if you have several buddies along. The cover doesn't always lend itself to that technique. In such cases, the normal thing is to form a line and work through the fields or whatever; however, again it will improve your flushing average if each hunter zigzags as he does, in effect creating a multiple-direction advance which at times will have several hunters moving toward each other, pinching birds between them, or angling in various directions simultaneously, which can again confuse pheasants which can't be sure what's going on. In cases like this, some birds will simply squat and hope to remain unseen, but others will flush in desperation and you'll get shooting. Obviously, proper gun handling techniques *must* be observed at all times, so no one does any shooting in a way that will endanger another hunter.

Whether pheasant shooting is difficult or not depends largely on the cover. If a rooster is flushed at close range in a weedfield or a low chopping, hitting him isn't too tough. Flushing speed isn't high and the target is big, so misses

On opening day, ringnecks are taken in easy cover like this—low cornfields, weedfields, etc. After they've been shot at a bit, they head for the jungles.

shouldn't be common. That's the kind of chance that's typical on opening morning of the season.

Shooting in tall standing corn is more difficult. If a bird rises ahead of you when you're driving, as soon as he levels off after takeoff he appears to be slanting downhill into the corn. This is an optical illusion because you're beneath the top of the corn, but it affects your shooting, as does the knowledge that he's going to vanish behind the tassels in a moment. So you have to shoot quickly, leading from below as on a station one high house Skeet bird. And then if you do connect, there can be a problem in finding him in that jungle of corn, especially if it's waist-high in weeds throughout. So get a good fix on the falling bird, estimate how many yards out he will fall, and count steps as you run out there, so you know you're starting to hunt at about the right place. Two or more hunters who see the shot should all get a visual fix; that way, the intersection of their paths as they hurry over should be close to the actual drop spot.

A stander at the end of a cornfield should position himself against a tree or whatever to break up his outline. Birds soon recognize hunters as enemies and will sometimes shift their flight paths to avoid one. Even more likely to cause a change of direction is movement by the blocker. More than once I've seen pheasants shift course when a hunter raised his gun long before the bird was within range, intending to "take good aim." That's a bad way to shoot a shotgun anyway, so avoid it. If a bird is flying toward you, wait motionless until it gets almost to the range at which you want to shoot, then shoulder the gun and fire instantly, as if you had just seen it. Occasionally it will be obvious that a driven bird is going to pass out of range to one side. There's nothing to be lost by movement now, unless birds are so plentiful that others may be expected from this cover before the drivers come out, so you might as well make a dash to try to get into range. Different times I've cut a chancy 50-yard shot down to an easy 35-yard one in this way. Most such decisions have to be based on common sense. If movement will definitely help your chances, move. You're going to do a lot of hunting, on average, for every shot obtained, so do everything possible to cash in on the ones you get. Incoming shots are easy if you shoot at the right time. The trick is to just swing up through them and hit the trigger as the bird goes out of sight behind the muzzle. Don't let them get too close. It's easier to kill cleanly at 35 yards than 15 and makes for better eating.

Once hunting pressure has forced pheasants into the thick stuff where you can scarcely work your way through, the shooting gets tougher. You might hear a bird go out but be unable to see him at all, or at most get only a fleeting glimpse as it disappears in the surrounding mess. I don't like shooting at invisible targets, but on rare occasions a rooster will vanish just as your finger slaps the trigger, your swing happens to overlay the bird's path, and some pellets happen to get through the foliage. After such a shot, listen intently. You might hear the bird hit the ground. Even if you don't, make a thorough search of the probable striking area. Once in awhile you'll find a bird you don't really deserve, though it's always a thrill to make such a shot.

Hit 'em Where It Works

Pheasants are big tough birds that take a lot of killing unless

(Above) When a rooster gets caught between two gunners in the open like this, he's easy. Sometimes so easy that everyone gets careless except him, and he cackles his way into the distance, leaving a couple of frustrated and disbelieving hunters cussing themselves and wondering what happened. It happens often.

(Below) Ringnecks often flush well out in open fields—when they fly at all. This one's well up there, but he was down a second or two later.

the brain happens to be hit by a stray pellet. Way too often, the shot charge is centered too far back for the head to figure at all in the pattern. The cockbird's long tail is mainly responsible for this. When a shot is taken quickly, as on an unexpectedly flushing rooster, a novice hunter tends to view the whole bird as his target and holds for the middle of it. As the tail makes up about half the length, a shot charge socked into the middle actually centers on the rear of the body, and this doesn't kill quickly. The best thing to do when this happens is shoot again, quickly. Otherwise you'll have hell's own time putting that bird in your coat. He'll die, but the foxes will eat him, not you. The best way to avoid such hits is to concentrate on the rooster's head when he flushes. The gleaming white neck ring makes a conspicuous target. Look at that, not the bird as a whole, swing through it and shoot with the gun still moving. You'll find that on close-flushing birds this system will concentrate most of the charge right on the head and neck, for instant kills. Stay completely away from the tail end. There's nothing vital back there.

If you do knock a bird down and see it scuttling away on the ground, don't hesitate. Shoot it again, right now. The only possible exception to this is when you have a topnotch retriever close at hand. Personally, I shoot 'em anyhow. I've lost birds in situations like this, one when we had three fine retrievers working on it within seconds. So don't put too much faith in your dog, even if he's damn good. At close range you can knock the head off a running rooster; if he's farther out, just shoot for the pile. Better a slightly shot up bird in the gamebag than a broken-wing runner in the brush.

As for pheasant-killing stuff, I tend to go with high velocity loads and at least 1⅛ ounces of shot, oftentimes 1¼ ounces. If shooting in ordinary cover, 7½s will go in the open barrel for the close flushes, 6s in the tighter choke. On rare occasions for late season shooting, when I felt certain most of the chances were going to be at long range, I've gone to 6s and short magnum loads using 1½ ounces of 4s. If I were restricted to just one load for these birds, it would be 1¼ ounces of 6s. In my guns, at least, this combination gives the best compromise between pattern density and penetration.

CHAPTER 9

Wild Turkey

TRADITION HAS IT that Ben Franklin wanted the wild turkey named our national emblem, rather than the bald eagle. I dunno if Ol' Ben said this seriously or tongue-in-cheek, or if he ever said it at all, but whatever the case, I'm glad it never came about. Not because the turkey isn't worthy. It's sure a hell of a lot smarter than the fish-eating baldie everyone is so concerned about these days. Anyone who has seen an old gobbler strutting in the sun-dappled woods, wings arced out and down till the feathers scrape gouges in the humus, magnificent chocolate-tipped tail spread, chest expanded and burst-

Bud Erich pauses while packing out a 20-pound gobbler to listen to another tom sounding off from the far ridge.

ing with bronze and iridescent highlights, beard dangling and those fantastically sharp eyes glittering from his wrinkled head as if to say, "Look at me, I'm king of this wild land!" has surely seen one of the most thrilling sights in the out-of-doors. But if the wild turkey had been named the national emblem, it obviously would not have an open season on it now, and sportsmen would miss some of the greatest hunting thrills ever.

There's some question whether the wild turkey should be classed as upland game or not. My own feeling is that it qualifies as big game, for in many ways it's more impressive than any small game or waterfowl I've ever hunted, yet it is often found in the same environment as grouse and most sportsmen use shotguns when hunting it, so I suppose we can stretch a point and include it here.

The wild turkey is an American bird. Before the European settlers arrived here, it was plentiful from southern Ontario down to Mexico, and the Spanish took these big birds home with them after their conquest of Mexico. The domestic turkey evolved from these and some were brought back to America by settlers in the 1500's. Wild birds were abundant here in those days, but their numbers decreased drastically as the country was settled and the ax and the plow destroyed their habitat. Turkeys are basically birds of wilderness or semi-wilderness areas, and they don't take kindly to civilization—another reason to admire them. Because of their comparatively large size and early abundance, they were an important food species for early settlers; that is, they were worth expending a powder charge and ball on, even in times when supplies of these were limited. In some areas, at least, they were numerous enough to be deliberately pursued by market hunters, though their cash value was often low. The elimination of tremendous forested regions during the late 1800's and early 1900's decimated the wild turkey population, but sportsmen-sponsored wildlife programs during the past half-century have paid for research, habitat improvement and stocking activities which have brought this great bird back in significant numbers in many states.

Turkeys belong to the species *Meleagris gallopavo*. There are five or six subspecies in America, the wild turkey usually being placed in the subspecies *silvestris*. Adult males attain a height of up to 3 feet and a length of 4 feet, including an 18-inch tail. Various respected references list maximum weights of big gobblers as 40 to 60 pounds, but I can't imagine a wild gobbler getting anywhere near that big. I've known several hunters who killed upwards of a hundred gobblers each, and I have several friends—wildlife biologists—who have worked with and studied wild turkeys for years, and all of these agree that a 20-pound gobbler is a big one and a 25-pounder a damn

Harvey Graybill blends into brush while calling, but likes a clear view toward probable turkey approach so he can swing gun. Camo clothing and ability to sit motionless are required for this method, as is use of a diaphragm caller, which doesn't require hand movement to operate.

Johnny Stewart is known for the electronic callers he builds and sells, but they aren't legal for turkeys in Pennsylvania, so he used a box caller to bring in this medium-size Cameron County gobbler.

big one. To say that some individual birds attain twice that weight is literally incredible to me. Wild hens normally weigh about half as much as gobblers, 8 to 10 pounds, and are about one-third shorter.

In dark woods, turkeys look almost black, but when the sunlight hits them their feathers gleam iridescently with green, copper and mahogany highlights. A gobbler's breast feathers are tipped with black, while those of the hen have a brown or buff tip. The gobbler has a beard on his chest, coarse hairlike feathers somewhat resembling a frayed tar-colored rope. It occasionally reaches a length of 10 or 12 inches, but because it is somewhat brittle the ends usually break or fray off before it grows this long. On rare occasions a gobbler will have two or three beards, and once in a great while a hen will grow one. The gobbler also has spurs on the back of his legs, bony spikes used for fighting. Turkeys' heads are practically bare, bluish-gray in color except during the breeding season when the gobbler's head and neck can be red, blue, purple or off-white, depending on his emotions of the moment.

Over the centuries, domestic turkeys have been bred for food, and they have a roundish meaty appearance due to the exaggerated breast and legs which supply the most edible portions. Wild turkeys have a rangier look to them. They are slimmer, with longer, snakelike necks, smaller heads and longer legs. The tail feathers and upper tail coverts of the eastern wild bird have chestnut-brown tips, while these are white on domestic turkeys.

Turkeys spend a lot of their time searching for food, covering perhaps several miles a day, scratching in the leaves and humus for whatever they can find. Depending on the time of year, they eat greens, tubers, shoots, grasshoppers, beetles, walking-sticks, spiders, centipedes, snails, seeds, fruits, roots, stems, flowers, leaves, acorns, beechnuts, etc. In winter, spring seeps provide some greens and insect larvae, and they scrounge for leftover seeds and nuts.

Turkeys are not long distance flyers like migratory birds, and like the ringneck they often prefer running to flying when startled. The bigger individuals sometimes seem to have trouble getting airborne, but once up they can attain a speed of 50mph, and it's not unusual for them to fly a mile or so—no mean feat when you consider the weight of these birds in relation to their wing area. On the ground, a big turkey can take 4-foot strides when frightened and will easily outrun a man in the woods. Once while hunting grouse in the early '50s, I flushed a small hen turkey at 35 yards or so—long-range on a bird that size for the field loads of 7½s my Browning Sweet 16 held. I heard those light pellets rattling off her feathers with every shot, but some got into the vitals and she planed down toward the bottom of the sidehill we were on and hit running. I was running, too, by that time, down the rocky, laurel-grown slope with an empty gun, which didn't particularly matter as she was way too far for my improved cylinder barrel. I was a lot younger then, and in pretty good shape after setting chokers for 2 years in an Idaho logging camp, but I never would have caught that young hen if it hadn't been for my dog. I don't know how many pellets got into the body, but it wasn't enough to make anyone worry about biting down after she came out of the roaster. Anyhow, I can tell you firsthand that what you're most likely to get from chasing a running turkey on foot is a broken leg, so if you go turkey hunting use more appropriate ammo or shoot them in the head.

Habitat and Breeding

Turkeys spend the nights in trees, a good-size flock often roosting close together. In cold weather they prefer conifers for the protection these give against the wind. There are exceptions, though. Last December, while climbing an old snow-covered logging road before dawn to reach a deer stand, I scared a big turkey out of the bare branches of a tall hardwood. Temperature at the time was in the low teens.

In spring, a gobbler's instinct turns toward reproduction. His wattles redden, he develops a fatty breast growth that will help sustain him during the breeding season, and he begins to gobble in early morning and evening. He struts proudly for the hens, head pulled back and chest distended, displaying his widespread tail and dragging his wingtips. It's not unusual for gobblers to fight each other while collecting eight or 10 hens into a sort of harem.

Fertilized eggs may be laid up to a month after mating, as the male turkey's sperm is stored in the hen's oviduct. One mating fertilizes the entire clutch. Impregnated females leave the flock to build a nest.

Turkey nests are little more than leaf-lined depressions in the ground, but they are usually carefully hidden by vegetation or a log, or they are backed up against the trunk of a tree. The hen lays an egg a day until she has produced a dozen or so, and she does the incubation herself. This takes about 28 days. Poults do not eat for 2 days after hatching, but move about almost immediately. Many predators prey on the eggs or poults, including snakes, minks, coons, opossums, crows and red squirrels. Sometimes the nesting hen is killed by a larger predator such as a fox or bobcat. Until old enough to fly up into trees for safety (about 2 weeks), poults have no defense against predators except hiding, and a lot of them don't make it to adulthood. In fact, average annual turkey mortality from all causes is about 70 percent. Nevertheless, enough survive to make hunting them one of the most challenging things a sportsman can try.

(Above right) Eric Wunz approaches a big gobbler he took in Centre County, Pennsylvania, profiting from the advice his dad gave him during the growing-up years.

(Right) Wildlife biologists Jerry Wunz and Bill Drake prove their turkey knowledge is based on firsthand information gained in turkey country. (Photo by Arnie Hayden.)

Dull-colored or camo clothing, gloves and face mask help hunter blend into background even when not actually concealed. However shiny gun can reflect light that will spook a wary gobbler. Camo tape such as bowhunters use will correct this problem easily and inexpensively.

Scoped smallbore rifle, such as a 22 WRF Magnum, 5mm Remington, 22 Hornet or 222, will handle turkeys well at woods ranges if shooter does his part.

Hunting and Its History

A number of states have two seasons on these big birds—the traditional fall season, usually occurring when various other species also are open to hunting, and a spring season. In the fall season any turkey—male or female, regardless of size—normally can be shot. The spring season, which is opened after the breeding activity ends, is for gobblers only. By this time they have done their bit toward perpetuating the species so the losses due to hunting have no negative effect on the overall population. The surviving poults more than replace the gobblers taken by hunters, so the old toms might as well provide recreation and food for sportsmen and their families.

Some decades ago, when the turkey population was lower and its range comparatively restricted, few sportsmen had the opportunity to hunt this magnificent bird. And not all of those who might have hunted him did so. Those who did, the ones who learned his habits and moods and actions and successfully hunted him on wild ridges and in lonely swamps, became a sort of hunter's elite, a select few who at least on a local or regional basis gained a stature that was unusual for their time. They were talked about by other hunters and acquaintances somewhat as our western gunfighters were in their day. A few of them wrote about their hunts. Archibald Rutledge is one who comes to mind, a wonderful outdoor writer of an earlier day. He once told me that in his lifetime—a long one, much of which was spent hunting—he had bagged upwards of 200 wild turkeys. His stories leave no doubt that he felt an old gobbler was one of the world's great trophies. Henry E. Davis was another. His book, *The American Wild Turkey,* is a hunting classic, not only for the information it presents about the bird but also—and perhaps mainly—because Davis was an extremely knowledgeable gun crank. His firsthand observations on the relative efficiency of vari-

A box caller is an excellent choice for anyone unable to use a diaphragm, but it's a good idea to use a log or other dense cover to shield hand movement which is necessary with this kind of call. Gun should always be close, as here, so it can be picked up as the call is laid down. (Photo by Joe Osman.)

ous shotguns and numerous small-caliber, high-velocity loads in both factory and custom rifles, and his comments on the scopes available in his day, make fascinating reading for anyone interested in firearms. I never knew him, but wish I had. It would have been great to talk with someone of his experience. Perhaps the most renowned turkey hunter of them all was Fleetwood Lanneau, a civil engineer and surveyor who lived in the heart of South Carolina's Great Pee Dee River swamps for 13 years and carried a rifle wherever he went. He reportedly killed between 300 and 400 wild turkeys with his rifles, many of them flying. His feats are the stuff of hunting legends. It's unlikely that anyone will ever again have the opportunity to do the kind of daily hunting in such a game-rich area as he did.

The Modern Turkey Hunter

Yet we have many fine turkey hunters now, men who almost religiously follow the seasons as they open, from Florida, Georgia and Alabama, up through the Carolinas and Virginias, Pennsylvania and New York. If their legal annual bag is limited to only one or possibly two birds in a given state, they still accumulate impressive numbers of birds because they hunt in so many states. Not that large bags in themselves are important, but they do indicate the magnetism the wild turkey has for dedicated hunters. Among these men must be included Pennsylvanians such as the late Louis Stevenson of Tioga County, who called in hundreds of birds for himself and friends; wildlife biologist Jerry Wunz, who has studied and hunted turkeys for many years; Roger Latham, outdoor editor of the *Pittsburgh Press* and author of *Complete Book of the Wild Turkey;* Bob Clark, executive director of the Pennsylvania Forestry Association; Harvey Graybill; the Rohm family of Perry County, Dale and his sons Robby, Terry and Jody; Wilson Moore and Rob Keck, outstanding callers all. There are many more, of course, here and in all

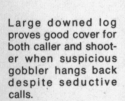

Large downed log proves good cover for both caller and shooter when suspicious gobbler hangs back despite seductive calls.

other states where the turkey is hunted. I mention these only because they are near-neighbors with whom I've had the chance to talk or hunt. And they are typical of the current generation of turkey hunters, men who have not only studied the data collected by earlier outdoorsmen—formal researchers as well as observant hunters—but also have added significantly to that store of knowledge. Anyone new to turkey hunting who wants to get off on the right foot would do well to obtain the books or articles written by some of the men mentioned above and study them thoroughly. Other publications of great value are Jim Brady's *Modern Turkey Hunting,* Dave Harbour's *Hunting the American Wild Turkey* and Tom Turpin's booklet "Hunting the Wild Turkey." Books aren't a complete substitute for actual experience, of course, but they can keep you from making a lot of mistakes early in the game, and during the off-season they bring back good memories and keep you in a hunting mood. Books devoted to this single species go into much detail on hunting methods and techniques; we'll just try to hit some highlights here.

Calling

Turkey hunting is different from most other types of hunting in that the usual method in either spring or fall seasons is to have the quarry come to you, rather than going to it. This might seem a passive thing, but it isn't. It requires preparation. To just go out into the woods and sit down on a stump, hoping an old gobbler will walk up and present himself for execution, isn't really the way to acquire a bird for the roaster. You could well have a long beard of your own—gray!—before one wanders within range. You usually have to make them come to you, and this is done by getting into turkey country and calling.

Four calls cover almost any situation: the hen's mating yelp, used to bring in spring gobblers; the kee-kee and the "lost" call, which are necessary in fall hunting; and the gobble, often used to locate roosting toms late in the day.

There are various kinds of callers, all available from a number of manufacturers, and a few do-it-yourselfers even make their own. The types most used are the *box caller,* which is the easiest to get good results from; the *diaphragm,* the most difficult to use until you get the hang of it; the *slate and peg;* the *yelper;* and the *flexible tube "gobbler."* There are other styles, plus variations on some of these, but these five will do everything necessary. Except for the diaphragm, a small thin unit used inside the mouth, all are worked or held by the hands, which means some motion is required, and this sometimes is seen by incoming birds. Also, when it's time to shoot, the hand-held types must be laid down, the gun picked up and aimed, and this, too, is motion that can cost you. The diaphragm has none of these problems, so it's the one preferred by many experts. It will make all of the calls normally necessary, including the gobble, though this is difficult, even for many who are skilled in its use. Nevertheless, I've heard Jerry Wunz and Rob Rohm do fine gobbles on a diaphragm caller.

Personal instruction by a *skilled* caller is the best way to learn how to use a call. If this isn't available, records are. After you know what to do, it's just a matter of practice. And more practice. And then getting out where the birds are.

If You're Just Starting . . .

A hunter who is starting from scratch doesn't even know where turkey country is, though. His best bet is to strike up an acquaintance with a turkey hunter or two at a local sportsman's club or claybird range. Not that anyone is likely to give away a special "private" area, but they will help out in general terms. A letter to the state game commission will also bring basic where-to-go information and kill-by-county re-

ports. These will at least get you into the right part of the state. The next step is scouting—when you narrow a general area down to a particular one. Wild creatures are not always in the same areas during hunting season as in summer, say, but it's a good idea to get out in different times of the year, so you can learn as much about this interesting species as possible. Summer scouting can be informative in itself, and this will naturally lead to more in early fall, when it will be most helpful for the upcoming season.

A significant percentage of the turkey's time is spent in finding food. This is true of most wild creatures, but too many hunters ignore the fact, perhaps forgetting that one of the main reasons they go to work 5 days a week is to feed themselves and their families. Turkeys avoid all the middlemen and go straight to the source themselves. So look at hunting areas critically, search for acorns, beechnuts, cherries, grapes, etc. When food is widespread, the game will be, too. When it's scarce, and thus concentrated in certain places, the birds will be concentrated, too. When these things are learned shortly before the fall hunting season opens, the best areas for hunting reveal themselves. Look for signs of the birds—scratchings, droppings, dusting spots, stray feathers, tracks in mud or snow. Listen for their sounds. Gobbling is the basis around which almost all spring turkey hunting is oriented, but old toms aren't completely silent the rest of the year. They gobble to some extent the year round. And all turkeys make various other sounds and calls. Furthermore, when a flock is feeding its way through the dry leaf cover typical of hardwood forests, it's sometimes possible to hear them scratching, just as you can hear nearby squirrels messing around. So scouting can be revealing, and it's definitely important.

Shotgun or Rifle?

When the fall season arrives and you know where turkey country is, you have to make a choice about the gun you're going to go with. At this time of year, rifles are usually legal as well as shotguns, which isn't generally true in the spring season. There are times when killing a wild turkey with a rifle is one of the great feats in Ameican hunting. Some of the swamp shooting described by Davis would fall into this category, and some day I hope to try it. However, there are many occasions when the use of a rifle rubs me wrong. To watch a snow-covered hillside of open woods known to be frequented by turkeys, and pot one at 200 or 300 yards when it hasn't the slightest reason to suspect there is any danger within miles, somehow doesn't seem fair to the turkey. I write this as a hunter who is primarily a rifleman rather than a shotgunner, one who at last count had nine scope-mounted varmint rifles ranging in size from a M52 Winchester sporter up to a heavy-barrel .25-06, and as a guy who would rather hunt woodchucks in the summer than eat. I know that killing a turkey at 300 yards can be difficult for even a topnotch rifleman under certain conditions. I also know there are times when it is child's play, and these are the shots I'm dubious about. However, I'm merely voicing an opinion here. Every hunter has to set his own standards for dealing with the game he hunts. If you prefer a good scoped rifle in the fall, and it's legal where you hunt, I have faith that you will use it in a sporting manner.

Choice of calibers can be tricky. If you read Davis's book, it's easy to conclude that the old .22 Hornet or K-Hornet, an ancient wildcat, would be near-perfect. For him, they were. But keep in mind that his shooting was done at comparatively short-range, mostly under 100 yards. At such distance, a 45-gr. HP or softpoint traveling at perhaps 2000 fps at impact, is almost perfect. Glenn Hoy, a hunting friend, has proved this to me in recent years by killing a dozen or so turkeys with his scoped 5mm Remington Rimfire Magnum, which uses a 38-gr. HP bullet at a muzzle velocity just over 2000 fps. When

In fall season, when turkeys can sometimes be seen at longer ranges than in spring, a combination gun can be just the ticket for long or short shots.

I once asked how it worked, he just grinned and said, "One shot and done. Just put it at the butt of the wing and squeeze." Bullet placement has the most to do with hunting success, and the butt of the wing is the spot to hit on broadside chances.

But the turkey that looks so big at 70 yards doesn't look quite that large at 300. And making such a precise hit—which really calls for sticking that bullet into a baseball-size target—is no simple thing, even with a 6x to 12x scope. The problem is greatly compounded by any movement of the target; the difficulty in knowing the precise range, which affects your aiming point; the lack of a solid shooting position, and all the other variables common to hunting that don't show up when testing loads on a benchrest.

Further problems result from the fact that the rifle/cartridge combinations most capable of delivering the requisite accuracy are the medium and bigger centerfire varmint loads—from the .222 up through the various 6mm's, say. These cartridges were designed to instantly kill woodchucks, gristle-hided, tough-meated, 7- to 12-pound critters. Few people eat chucks so it doesn't matter how badly the bullet tears them up. However, when you turn such loads loose on turkeys, results can be depressing. Nevertheless, these are the kinds needed for success when the ranges get beyond 150 yards or so. They're the only ones, outside of the even more destructive high-velocity big game cartridges, which have the accuracy and flatness of trajectory to make hits likely.

Full choke ribbed barrels that can be aimed almost like a rifle are the preferred armament for called-in gobblers. Most hunters prefer 12 gauges and heavy loads of medium-size shot for such shooting. The first shot, at least, is deliberately placed on the head and neck area. If put there, the kill is instantaneous.

In the fall season, a flying gobbler can provide sudden excitement for a grouse hunter. For a clean kill, his charge of 7½s better be centered on the head.

To reduce meat destruction, it's commonly recommended that non-expanding bullets be used. This sounds good, but it doesn't always work. The breast meat of a turkey has an unusual consistency that tends to splatter when hit by a high-velocity bullet, even if the bullet doesn't expand. In the end, the only way you can hope not to destroy a lot of meat with a rifle is to miss the eating parts completely. That's difficult enough when the bird is broadside, almost impossible when standing end-on. High-velocity bullets don't merely put a caliber-size hole through a critter. They usually create a cone-shaped volume of destroyed tissue with destructive shock waves radiating outward even further. So, much as I admire the efficiency of such outfits on varmints, I'm dubious about their use on turkeys under most conditions.

All of which leaves the shotgun as the most practical firearm for turkeys. Most veteran hunters agree that a tight-patterning choke and medium shot, size 6, 5, or 4, make the top combination. The 6s are usually chosen to give the densest pattern (of these sizes) when shooting birds brought in by the call. Since this is how most gobblers are bagged, this size probably accounts for most. Ofttimes, the hunter will use heavier pellets for follow-up loads in a repeater. This is on the assumption that the bird will then be escaping and the head-neck area—which should always be the target on an incoming gobbler—won't be readily offered to the shot. From the side or rear, heavy feathers, bones and thick meat guard the vitals, so penetration is a necessity and larger shot is required.

Because the head-neck target is small, even at close range, it's important that the gun throw its pattern exactly where you expect it to. Many guns don't. Not all shotgun shooters are aware of that fact. Most deer hunters realize they have to zero in their rifles annually, and all experienced varmint shooters know that for consistent hits on their small, long-range targets their zeros must be verified regularly, but most shotgunners have never thought of the possibility that their patterns might not be going right where they point the muzzle. The size of the pattern in the 25-40 yard bracket where most small game is shot tends to conceal the fact, the edge of the spread often connecting. But if the target were smaller, like a gobbler's head, for instance, this fringe of pellets might not do the job. So put up a target at short range, 10 or 15 yards, and with the back of the forward hand rested on something to steady things, put the front sight on the aiming point and squeeze off a couple of shots with each of several kinds of ammo. The results might surprise you. If the center of the pattern is where you want it, good. Or if it's close enough and consistently placed, okay. But if it's way off, you'd better do some stock altering. That'll help on small game, too. This is particularly important on turkeys because you normally aim the first shot like a rifle, and you want the pattern to smother the head-neck area.

Single barrel guns are usually pretty good in this respect, but doubles, particularly the less expensive side-by-sides, can give some sorry surprises. They don't always shoot where you're pointing, and it's common to have the pattern from each barrel center on a different point of impact—in other words, not overlap. It's better to find this out on a sheet of newspaper than on a gobbler.

You can't trust the choke designation marked on a barrel, either. With a given shell, a tube marked "full" might give modified patterns, or vice versa, yet be correct with a different kind of ammo or a different size of shot. So get at least a small assortment of shells and do some serious testing. You can cut down the cost by trying this with a couple of friends, as it doesn't require a full box to show how any particular combination works in one gun. Sometimes you learn some pleasant things. Example: Bob Wise's O/U Franchi 12-gauge, marked improved cylinder and modified, does give IC patterns with 7½s, but with one make of 5s he gets super-full patterns out of the modified tube, thus has an ideal combination for late season pheasants, when most shots are either close or way out. But you don't know such things unless you do some experimenting.

One other thing on guns. A highly polished one reflects sunlight like a mirror, and quite likely scares off more incoming gobblers than everything else put together. It's bad enough when motionless, much worse when you move it, as you probably must in order to get on target. Camouflage tape is cheap, so get some. (Archery shops sell it; those bowhunters ain't dumb, and they're trying for whitetails at ranges similar to those where gobblers are taken. If a deer is spooked by a flash of reflected sunlight, what do you think it'll do to an old gobbler?)

Best Methods for Bagging Turkey

Probably the conventional way to hunt turkeys in the fall, at least for a competent caller, is to find a bunch of birds, frighten them into scattering in all directions, then hide at that spot and call. They want to reassemble, but that doesn't mean you have easy pickings. If even one of those sharp-eyed critters sees something unnatural—and now a lot of 'em are looking—they'll all be gone. Perhaps the best time to break up the flock is just before dark one day, which means they will roost separately and be anxious to get together the following morning, when you'll be there with your call. The guys who know tell me the *"lost"* call and the *kee-kee* run are the best to try in the fall.

Other fall hunters sort of still-hunt for turkeys—move slowly on foot through areas which scouting has indicated holds birds. The objective is to get within range of a magnum

(Above and below) Not much cover here, but sometimes you get caught in such places, and if you're good enough with a call — as Jerry Wunz is — you might have as big a bird to show for your efforts as he does.

shotgun charge, say, or perhaps a scoped .222. This is one of the hardest chores a hunter can cut out for himself. A wild turkey has eyes that see everything—not only a moving hunter such as a whitetail buck would spot, but a motionless, camouflaged hunter that nothing else might spot. This isn't to say the turkey will always recognize a still, inconspicuous figure as a hunter, but he'll see it. I remember one frosty spring morning in Tioga County when Lou Stevenson was calling for me and a young bird was coming. We were in a fairly open woods, in a little cover and backed up against adjacent trees. We were wearing full camo including facemasks. When I saw the turkey come out of some trees, it was out of range—maybe 65 yards distant. I froze absolutely motionless, even holding my breath, watching it approach. It moved alertly, but didn't seem overly suspicious as Lou was a great caller. But by the time it had covered another 20 yards, I simply had to breathe. Normally that would have been no problem, but as I said, the morning was frosty in those northern mountains, and every breath made a cloud. I exhaled as slowly as possible, hoping the facemask would dissipate the condensed vapor, and I guess it did somewhat for only minute traces seemed to drift away. But that was enough. The bird froze, too, motionless as a stump, little head zeroed in on me like a rifle sight. He was still too far to shoot; in fact, I wasn't certain he was a legal target as in Pennsylvania's spring season a turkey must have a beard and I couldn't see one from this distance. I never did find out, either, for when simple survival made me dribble out another breath, that bird simply departed. Young, he might have been, but stupid he wasn't, and when his fabulous eyes picked up something just slightly suspicious, he vanished. For all I know, he's still wandering those steep ridges, sending his gobbles echoing through the hollows every spring. I hope so.

I guess it isn't impossible to still-hunt within range of a turkey, as I've gotten that close to an occasional bird when mooching for deer and I'm certain many others are quieter than I am in the woods. However, I'd expect that a moving hunter's best chance is to try to see unalarmed turkeys before they spot him, which can be well beyond any sensible shooting distance, then outflank them and take a stand where they might feed into him.

In early spring, the reproductive urge starts working on the gobblers and each one establishes his own territory where he struts and gobbles to attract as many hens as possible, and fights with other males that intrude on his area. This gobbling is done just before and after an old tom leaves his roost, which is usually about daybreak. And it is by way of the gobbling that the spring hunter locates his turkey. He's in the general area before dawn. In a state like Pennsylvania, where countless dirt roads snake through the forested regions, he cruises slowly, stopping the car often to listen for the gobble which the tom intends only for some receptive hens. In more genuine wilderness areas, he hikes cross-country, listening and sometimes using the hen's mating yelp to entice a gobble if he hears none. A gobble can be heard a long ways on a still morning, over a mile when conditions are right, and the hunter tries to pinpoint the location of any he hears. This is where familiarity with the area gained through previous scouting can be helpful. If a hunter is passing through turkey country in late afternoon or early evening, he can sometimes get a response by gobbling. A tom on the roost will often be upset by the idea that another male is in his territory and gobble angrily in return. The man notes as closely as possible the spot where the gobbles are coming from. The bird will be in that general area for some time to come, as it's the territory he has claimed for this breeding season.

Almost any sharp unexpected noise, such as the slamming of a car door, will sometimes bring a gobble. The call of an owl

Results of a good morning in Venango County, Pennsylvania. From left, Ben Rodgers Lee, guide Bob Lambert, John Hood, George Jamison and Bud Guilinger. (Photo by Bob Parlaman.)

often brings a response from a bird. However, this ploy works best in areas of few hunters. Some places are so overrun with would-be turkey shooters, all calling, hooting and slamming, that the real birds refuse to respond to anything, doubtless scuttling for distant swamps with silent 4-foot strides when the racket gets going. It's best to avoid such crowded places, of course. Besides the obvious problems, the whole tone and setting is wrong.

There's always a chance that someone else will be working on a given bird the first morning of the season, so you should

This gobbler is bigger than it looks in comparison to Ben Rodgers Lee, a big fellow and one of the all-time great turkey callers. (Photo by Bob Parlaman.)

have a backup available. And you don't want it to be so far away that all your hunting time is wasted on travel. In spring, it's customary for shooting hours to end at noon or earlier, to avoid disturbing nesting hens, so you don't have all day to hunt.

Let's assume you've learned something about calling, have done your pre-season scouting, have located a couple of gobblers, and the country isn't overcrowded. What now? Well, comes that first morning of the spring season, the first thing to do is get up early. Awfully early. Because you've gotta get dressed, eat breakfast, drive to wherever you're going, quietly walk to within a couple hundred yards of the tree you believe your gobbler is roosting in, and be settled down, motionless and quiet, well before first light. Then you wait. You don't sneeze, or cough, or blow your nose. You don't decide to move in closer. You don't mess with your gun. (You loaded it earlier, after you first got in the woods, put the safety on and checked it. Now you don't mess with it. It'll work when the time comes.) You don't do anything but wait.

After you've sat there forever, you suddenly realize that the blackness is sort of gray. Then the sounds of the dickeybirds begin to drift through the stillness, and the cast of the eastern sky is paler. The tension begins to build up inside you. You haven't heard anything real, but you know the second hand of the hunter's clock is sweeping toward zero. Even in the chill air, your palms are starting to sweat against the gun's stock. Suddenly, there it is—*Gilobble-obble-obble! Gilobble-obble-obble!*— the heart-jamming gobble of a wild turkey knifing through the pre-dawn stillness. It sends a chill up your spine, makes your breath catch, raises the hackles on your neck. There's no other sound like it. It doesn't have the mystery of invisible Canada geese calling in the night, doesn't bring the exhilaration of an elk's bugle in Chamberlain Basin's black timber. It simply dominates the forest, loud, bold, overpowering. In your mind's eye you can see that big old gobbler as plainly as if it were high noon and he was scarcely a dozen steps ahead of you—which is precisely where you hope he'll soon be.

You don't move. You don't call. You listen. That first gobble probably came from the roost tree. Maybe the next one will. But you know he'll be leaving there any moment

This isn't an invader from outer space, but merely a camouflaged turkey hunter awaiting an incoming gobbler. His chances of escaping detection would be still better if he wore gloves and used camo tape on his Ithaca.

now, unless he thinks a hen might be coming his way—which is why you don't do any yelping yet. You listen harder. Minutes pass. He doesn't gobble again. Then you hear it, the rustling sound of the big bird leaving his roost and landing maybe 100 yards below you. Your blood pressure goes up another notch. You're glad you picked a stand that put you above him. Gobblers are more likely to come uphill than down, you know. *Maybe you really have a chance,* you suddenly think. Somehow that never quite seemed possible. Even when you were asking all those questions, and working with the call, and scouting, it was all sort of abstract, a vague, sometime-in-the-future possibility. But now, right now, here you are, alone in honest-to-God turkey woods with a gun in your hands, and right down there, maybe within the length of a football field, is an honest-to-God wild turkey. The enormity of it all suddenly overpowers you. There's an urge to shout, to get up and run away. You shove that foolishness behind you, not even taking time to ridicule yourself for such reactions; you're a turkey hunter, you've got things to do.

Forcing yourself to remain calm, you tell yourself you're going to make three soft yelps on your caller. He's not far away, you don't want to be loud, he'll hear you no matter how quiet you are. Nervously but silently you prepare the box caller. You wish you could use a diaphragm, it would be so much simpler. But you can't. A trickle of sweat rolls down your temple and your hands are damp. You force yourself to relax. You can do it. You've done it thousands of times at home. The edges are chalked now, you—your heart lurches as the lid touches the box edge, brings a tiny *yik,* and you squeeze it against you almost hard enough to crush it, heart hammering. Did he hear it! God! You sit there, catatonic, mouth open, breath held, straining to hear anything from down there. But there's nothing. Slowly, the overpowering numbness lessens and you finally feel your blood begin to circulate again.

You gain courage. Your movements are decisive. You grasp the box, hesitate, then stroke it three times. Perfect! The yelps drift tremulously away. You're done. You lay the caller aside. Nothing in Heaven or Earth could make you pick it up again. That was it, win, lose or draw.

Almost before the sound fades, there's an answering gobble and the gun is in your hands. You can't remember picking it up, but its checkering is biting your palms. Where is he!

Again that urge to do something crazy. But it's easier to fight down this time. You wait. Silent as a stone. Somewhere down there, proud as Tut, he's listening, too, expecting you to come to him, diffidently, perhaps, but unable to help yourself. After all, he's the emperor here, proud, probably strutting—yes, there it is, another blasting gobble! He's mad. His hen isn't playing the game. She's supposed to come to him. Well, he'll show her . . .

You wait. Minutes pass. Has he vanished like the mist in the rising sun? You look at the caller, lying there so mutely. If only you had the confidence to stroke it again. Before next year . . . But now it's this year. Maybe he's coming, you think. When the gobbling stops, that often means they're coming. You ease the gun up, slower than an oozing glacier, grateful you took time to tape it. Your eyes ache from searching. For a moment there . . . No, nothing. Just your eyes playing tricks among the shadows. You wonder if you should look away, not concentrate so hard; relaxation will give you a wider field of view, if only . . . There he is. Absolutely nothing, then right there, almost straight in front of your gun, strutting like a—like an old turkey gobbler! There he is, tail fanned, wingtips dragging, head pulled back and chest extended, the struttin'est old tom on the mountain.

Almost subconsciously you check the distance, realize he's well inside the 30-yard tree you picked out at dawn, and ease the gun's front sight onto his neck. Your finger moves with a will of its own and from somewhere in the vast distance you faintly hear the gun's boom. And then you're racing toward that great wing-fanning bird that's flopping in the leaves, and you grab him and hold him and when the last reflexive actions subside you lift him high and smooth his beautiful iridescent feathers and slowly realize you've done it, you've done it all, you're a turkey hunter at last.

And then you mutter: "My God, there are men who have lived this hour a hundred times."

CHAPTER 10

The Gun and Its Use

IF THE UPLAND HUNTER were truly a rational creature, it would be easy to choose a gun to serve his needs. He would simply buy one that handles ¾-ounce or more of shot well and go hunting. It wouldn't matter in the slightest who manufactured the gun, whether it was a slide action, autoloader, side-by-side or over-under, or even if it happened to be a single shot. He could kill well with any of them—maybe best of all with the single shot as the knowledge that success or failure hinges on the shell in the chamber rather than on those

Foliage is gone when the winter grouse season arrives, but Chuck Fergus has learned from experience that his little 280 Ithaca 20-gauge will still reach out far enough to do the job.

in the magazine tends to make the shooter put that shell's shot charge where it should go.

But as with fly fishermen, trapshooters and others of similar ilk, no one ever accused an upland hunter of being rational. When it comes to guns for his sport, he doesn't think, he feels. His actions, at bottom, are emotional, not logical. Oh, he can give all sorts of reasons for choosing whatever gun he carries, reasons that seem based on facts, and he can quote all sorts of ballistics, shooting authorities, reference books dating back almost to Chaucer (the English have *always* been noted for their "best quality" doubles!), etc., but the fact remains that once an upland hunter has a gun that will handle ¾-ounce of shot he doesn't actually need any other particular gun if his only goal is to kill grouse, pheasants or whatever. If the gun's stock is short enough that it can be easily shouldered and swung, and long enough that the shooter's thumb doesn't whack him in the nose, he can learn to shoot it well. That must be true, for over the centuries shotguns have varied tremendously in design, profile, etc.—any dimension you want to quote—yet at any given time there were true experts in their use. Obviously, shooting styles must differ with gun styles, yet so far as results are concerned—hitting the targets that are being shot at—things haven't changed significantly in generations. Sometimes it seems that the whole thing is a matter of fashion with a few individuals in any period having a perhaps undeserved influence on the whole field.

Be that as it may, we live and shoot in the here and now, and some conclusions about guns have been accepted by most experienced upland gunners. Some are definitely valid. No one who has fought his way through sidehill briar patches, mucky sloughs, grapevine tangles and weed-grown cornfields to kick out a ringneck, or who has hiked seemingly endless wooded mountain ridges trying to flush a grouse, would deny that a short, lightweight, fast-handling gun is preferable to a 32-inch cornsheller that tops 9 pounds when fully loaded. So where does that general statement leave us? Let's look at some specifics.

The guns are the glamour items, the things we all like to talk about and read about and, if you're a gunwriter, write about. But the truth is, the gun is just the tool that makes it possible to utilize a shotshell; it's the shell—the shot charge—that actually does the killing. So when thinking about an outfit for upland hunting, the first consideration really should be the shell.

Shot Shells and Loads

As mentioned, any gun that handles a minimum of ¾-ounce of shot well will handle most upland chances. This means a 28-gauge or larger. I know that the 3-inch .410 is supposed to

The M37 Ithaca is a popular slide action which loads and ejects through a port in the bottom of the action. A longtime favorite of the author.

(Below) Jim Bashline's pet, a Grade 1½ Ithaca restocked to his dimensions with Miller single trigger. A 12-gauge, its 26-inch barrels are both choked improved cylinder. It's an unbeatable grouse and woodcock gun and will easily handle close-flushing ringnecks.

carry this much shot, and possibly it does, but I've never seen one that handled it well, and that's an important difference. Cramming that much shot into the .410's long skinny case does nothing to help patterns; in fact, some veteran shooters who for their own reasons choose to use the .410 often pick the ½-ounce load in the 2½-inch case, feeling they benefit more from its better patterns than they do from the heavier charge in the long case. All things considered, I feel that the .410 is an expert's gun only, not a beginner's. It takes an awful lot of skill to overcome the built-in deficiencies of this little case, so don't give one to a youngster or a small woman on the assumption that its light recoil will help them. The missing and crippling they'll probably do will likely destroy any interest they might have in hunting.

The 28-gauge would be a better choice for a beginning hunter. It handles shot charges of ¾-, ⅞- or 1-ounce, and is probably at its best with the ⅞-ounce charge. That's just as well, for the heaviest load is not readily available in some areas. In fact, 28-gauge guns themselves are not seen in every grouse cover—a slightly sad fact, perhaps, but one that must be acknowledged. In recent years there has been a slight swell of interest in this gauge, and the popular Remington M1100 autoloader and M870 pump are chambered for it, as well as imported models such as the Franchi autoloader and the Browning Superposed. Still, when the average American gunner thinks of a small gauge it's the .410 he picks. (A dubious choice, not only because of the 28's ballistic superiority but also because the .410 is not truly a gauge but rather a caliber.)

I've never owned a 28-gauge, but have had a little experience with one. Some years ago I acquired several cases of Federal 28-gauge shells carrying ⅞-ounce of 7½ shot. I borrowed a Remington 1100 and one afternoon Dad and I shot them up on claybirds, some thrown from a hand trap, the rest from a Trius. It was a delightful and enlightening afternoon. With the fast handling 1100, hand-thrown birds and doubles out of the Trius were easy, but the most interesting part was letting a single get out as far as possible before shooting. The full-choked Remington must have been throwing beautiful patterns, for we could consistently break birds to 35 yards or so. That means the little 28 will handle all normal upland game shooting for most chances here are well under that range.

That's about as far as 7½ shot will give the penetration needed on pheasants anyway. Number 6 is better in that regard, but the pattern is considerably less dense, so it's doubtful that switching to the larger shot would be much advantage in the 28.

Once you get above the 28—to the 20-, 16- or 12-gauge—there's no problem. All will handle 1 to 1¼ ounces of shot, though it takes the 3-inch Magnum to do that in 20-gauge, and you can go to 1½ ounces in the 2¾-inch 12, if that seems necessary. The 3-inch 12-gauge can deliver an even heavier shot charge, but there's almost no reason for the upland hunter to go that route. A gunwriter of my youth, Bob Nichols of *Field & Stream*, once said that a hunter had to be an awfully fine shotgunner to utilize more than an ounce of shot. What he meant was that an ounce of 6s or 7½s would kill cleanly at any range where the average gunner could consistently connect, and that the efficiency of the heavier charges could be taken advantage of only by true experts. Nichols knew more than a little bit about shotgunning, and that statement proves it. An ounce of 6s will average four to six pellets in a broadside pheasant at 50 yards, the number depending on the choke through which its fired, and that's normally enough to down a

Chuck Fergus, the author and Wes Bower admire a long-tailed rooster taken on a foggy November day. All prefer doubles — a pair of O/U's and one S/S — for their fast-handling qualities and the instantaneous choice between two chokes — something no repeater can give.

(Right) Pigeons make great off-season targets. They're often found around stone quarries in warm weather. Besides shooting practice, they give the Lab a chance to do what it likes best — retrieving. This is Sam and the guy she lives with, Jim Bashline.

full-grown ringneck. An ounce of 7½s will put five to eight pellets in the bird at the same distance, but this smaller size doesn't always have the required penetration on a tough old rooster. Number 5 shot has significantly better penetration but fewer pellets, so patterns become sketchy with open chokes; it's a good choice for long shots from a full choke, though.

We've been talking only of 1-ounce loads here, but it's easy to get 1⅛ or 1¼ ounces in the three common gauges. These are deadlier, as the heavier charges are commonly loaded to slightly higher velocities than the 1-ounce, and of course you have more pellets working for you. But the difference is probably not as great as many hunters think. They might get a psychological boost from the knowledge their 3-inch 20s are stuffed with magnums, and shoot with more confidence because of the mental attitude, but the fact remains there isn't an overpowering difference between the shells. Obviously, a 1¼-ounce charge is 25 percent heavier than a 1-ounce charge, but if four pellets from the lighter load hit a bird, the 1¼-ounce load, on average, will put only five pellets in it—an increase of one pellet. There are times that can be important, but most of the time it isn't. (I know it can be a bit depressing to realize that the highly ballyhooed advantage of a magnum amounts to just one measly shot pellet, but that's how things go sometimes. It's also discouraging to realize that the velocity advantage of maximum loads, perhaps 200 feet per second at the muzzle, has dwindled to about 70 foot seconds at 40 yards, where the bird might be hit, but that too is a fact.)

What this all boils down to is that for upland shooting, where the vast majority of kills are made at under 35 yards, field loads carrying an ounce of 6s or 7½s will handle things well. A true expert can go with slightly lighter charges as he will center his patterns better, and the heavier high velocity loads will add some extra efficiency if it seems necessary or if a high percentage of shots must be taken in the 35-50 yard bracket. The average gunner, though, is advised to pass up the 50-yard stuff; that's really a long ways to try killing anything with a shotgun. Anyone who doubts this is invited to measure off 50 yards—genuine 3-feet-to-the-yard yards—and see how far it looks across his shotgun's muzzle. The vast majority of gunners will swear it's 70 yards or more, if unaware of the actual distance. Fact is, most hunters who kill a bird at 35 yards think it's 50. That might be good for their ego, but it has little relation to reality.

Different Loads for Different Upland Game

Different upland species require different loads for optimum results. Doves, woodcock and quail require far less energy to kill than grouse or pheasants. Their small size makes dense patterns necessary, so the gunner should choose smaller shot sizes, 7½, 8 or 9 being typical. An ounce load is usually more than sufficient for quail and woodcock, though doves, because they are often shot—or shot at—much farther, are downed more consistently with heavier loads. The added pellets are not needed for the energy, but rather to increase pattern density. A dove is a small bird even from the visual standpoint when you see the feathers; as a target, when those feathers don't count, its vital area is so tiny that it can be right in the middle of a 50-yard pattern and completely escape damage. So the more pellets you send after him, the better your chances are for a grill full of breasts on the charcoal burner some nippy fall afternoon. I usually use 1⅛ ounces of 7½s or 8s for these targets, and some friends go to 1¼ ounces.

Grouse are much larger birds and almost always are shot at shorter ranges than are doves—more like woodcock. An ounce of 7½s is a reasonable choice for this great game bird, with perhaps 1⅛ ounces useful for the second barrel or following loads in a repeater. These heavier loads would not be necessary if the shooting were done in the open, but in typical grouse cover—still heavily leafed during the early seasons and often a thick, dense jungle even after the frosts—significant percentages of a shot charge may be absorbed by intervening shrubbery, so it pays to have some extra pellets going out.

Pheasants are by far the toughest upland birds to kill, so the heavier loads should be first choice for this gaudy long-tailed critter. Early in the season, when shots average closer and birds of the year are not usually big, 1⅛ ounces of 7½s will handle the flushing shots, or those in thick cover, with the same weight of 6s for follow up chances. If a lot of hunting is done in weedfields, cornfields, or other areas where wild flushing or long crossing shots are common, 1¼ ounces of 6s will prove better. On a mathematical basis, there doesn't seem to be a lot of difference between 1⅛ and 1¼ ounces of shot, and actually there isn't. But in a practical sense, on long chances at these big tough birds, the slight edge of the heavier load becomes significant a surprising number of times. In early winter, when even birds of the year have reached full size and many shots are near maximum range, I've sometimes gone to short-magnum loads—1½ ounces of 6s kicked out by a 4 dram equivalent powder charge—for the tight barrel with good results.

Cottontails are comparatively easy to kill. They tend to be taken at short range, either ahead of the beagles or kicked out of their squats, and they're not too tenacious of life. A number of times I've seen them die quickly when struck by only one pellet in the body. This isn't typical, of course, but it does suggest that they aren't tough targets. It isn't typical, either, for a shotgun target to be hit by only one pellet, so the case doesn't come up often. An ounce or so of 7½s will handle most any rabbit shooting, though in winter seasons, when they can sometimes be seen at surprisingly long ranges as they run ahead of the dogs, a heavier load of 6s makes sense.

Squirrels are rifle game in my opinion, yet I'm sure that far more are killed by shotgunners than by hunters carrying precision-type scoped rifles. I'm not criticizing the use of shotguns here. A squirrel scrambling through the oak tops or scuttling through crisp brown leaf cover on the ground is as tough to hit as any rabbit and noticeably tougher to kill. If I were deliberately going after squirrels with a smoothbore, I'd stoke it full of 6s. In the limited number of bushytails I've taken with a shotgun while primarily hunting other species, 6s seemed deadlier than the 7½s I normally had in the other barrel.

That more or less covers the ammo situation for upland critters. Boiled down, it means a 1-ounce load of 7½s or 6s will handle most shots well, with 1⅛ or 1¼ ounces giving added efficiency for the longer or tougher shooting. Smaller shot, 8s or 9s, can be useful on woodcock, quail, and sometimes doves, and under certain conditions heavier shot, 5s or 4s, will be appropriate on pheasants.

Choosing the Right Gun

Some pages back it was suggested that any gun which handles ¾-ounce or more of shot well will handle most upland shots well, and that's true. However, hunters don't choose their smoothbores simply for mechanical or objective reasons. Most of us want a gun we can take some pride in, one that will give us satisfaction just in the handling of it at odd moments in the den between seasons as well as in the field in November, a gun we can show to hunting pals without apologizing. It doesn't have to be the most expensive in the world—obviously, not everyone can have a matched pair of Purdeys to use on the odd and even days of the week (and even if we had such treasures it's doubtful that we'd be willing to lug them into the greenbriars after late season roosters)—yet we'd all like to have a good quality shotgun. If this weren't true, we'd all be lugging inexpensive long barrel single shots. Many hunters start their careers with such an outfit and it invariably serves well. Yet somewhere along the way most move on to other types, Ol' Faithful being relegated to backup position or passed on to another shooter. Most hunters want a repeating shotgun, one that can be fired several times without taking the gun down to reload, and this is a reasonable feeling. Game birds are often missed or only wounded with the first shot, a covey or flock flushes or passes within range, so the advantages of a gun which can quickly deliver more than one shot are obvious. Let's take a quick look at the basic types.

The oldest way of supplying an immediate second shot is by use of a second barrel. This solution dates back to muzzle-loading days, and this design, which can be in either side-by-side or over-under configuration, in its ultimate form is probably the greatest example of the shotgun maker's art. (Three-and four-barrel guns—not the German drilling or vierling combination guns but true shotguns—have also been made from time to time, but these are so scarce they're of no importance here, if anywhere, except as *tours de force* or collectors' items.)

A double gun (this little L.C. Smith belonged to the author's father) makes it easy to use shells of different shot sizes to best handle both the close- and wild-flushing birds. The author likes 7½s in the open tube and 6s in the tight-choked barrel for most upland game.

(Left) Ray Johns has found the M500 Mossberg slide action a highly dependable outfit and especially likes it for long-range doves.

Around the turn of the century, during the days of much game and few restrictions on bag limits, even more firepower than the double offered was desired. Designers responded with single barrel repeaters which utilized large capacity tubular magazines hung beneath the barrel. Through either hand power or the use of waste power, created when a shell was fired, the empty case was ejected, the gun's firing mechanism was cocked, and a new shell loaded into the chamber. Early hand-operated examples, largely forgotten now, were the M1887 and M1901 Winchester lever actions, and the M1893, Winchester's first slide action. This was followed by the exceedingly popular M97 Winchester, and later the M1912, one of the all-time greats in the smoothbore field. It was also in this period that John Browning developed his outstanding autoloading shotgun, still produced and known as the Auto-5, the name reflecting the fact that it is unnecessary to manually operate the action and that the gun's capacity is five shells.

Despite the continuing popularity of lever action rifles, lever action shotguns have long faded from the scene and now are of interest to collectors and arms students only. However, double barrel, slide action, and autoloading shotguns are being made and sold in increasing numbers each year. There are many variations in technical design details—enough that large books have been written on such subjects—but these are not of great interest to most shotgunners. Nevertheless, some general comments might be helpful to new hunters.

Double barrel shotguns were popular in this country before the turn of the century, but the advent of single barrel repeaters led American gunners down another path. For generations, the slide action and autoloading designs were those most often seen in the uplands. There were various reasons for this. One was economics. It'd always been less expensive to get a high-grade repeater than a high-grade double. The former could be turned out by mass production methods, while a good double, whose twin barrels sometimes need hand regulation if they are to properly superimpose their patterns at a selected distance, require skilled personal attention.

The repeaters of course have virtues of their own which make them excellent choices for hunting. As mentioned, the large magazine capacity was important in days when game was more plentiful and legal limits larger. Now there is sometimes a tendency to list this design feature as something a game hog might prefer. I feel that's poor judgment. Large bags were perfectly legitimate in earlier days, and skilled hunters who made part of their living off of a renewable resource such as game had nothing to be ashamed of. They were a respected part of that day's society. Just because the situation has changed and their day has passed does not mean we should judge them by current standards. To fit into today's picture, a three-shell limit—one in the chamber and two in the magazine—is legally required for repeaters when hunting most game. Some are made to accept only that many shells, while the rest are easily reduced to it by means of a magazine plug inserted in the magazine tube itself.

The single barrel design, because it is presented as a narrow line extending forward from the shooting eye, is felt by many to point more precisely than the double barrel, which obviously appears as a wider unit. Many hunters, particularly those who do a significant percentage of their shooting at the longer ranges and perhaps have a more deliberate—almost aiming—method of firing, are convinced the single barrel is advantageous for them. They like not only the precision of the single barrel but also the added length which comes with the basic design. For a given barrel length, a repeater of course is some 4 to 6 inches longer than a double, a result of the gun's action being fitted between the barrel and stock. One effect of this is to move the gun's center of gravity forward, taking

Many hunters look down on a single shot gun, but countless pieces of upland game are taken with them each season. When a hunter knows he has but one load to do the job, he tends to put that one where it will do the most good. There's a moral in that somewhere. (Photo by Joe Osman.)

away some liveliness of feel but making for a smooth swing once it is put into motion.

A pump or autoloader also has a good hand-filling fore-end, something easy for the shooter to get a firm grip on, and it's located far enough forward to provide a natural position for the front hand. Such a fore-end is a necessity of design with the pump gun—it's actually the operating handle and wrapping it around the magazine tube requires a size that's naturally comfortable to the shooter. The fore-end on an autoloader doesn't have all the same functions, but since it does have to be big enough to enclose various working parts, it too makes a fine hand-filling unit. As a result, gun pointing with the front hand is helped, as is recoil absorption, since that hand really has something to clamp down on.

Single barrel repeaters also have another design feature that was non-existent on early double barrels—a single trigger. Obviously, if only one shell is available for firing at a given moment, only one "go" button is necessary. Besides elimi-

Don Lewis compares a M500 Ithaca SKB 12-gauge with 30-inch tubes — a pet goose gun — with 26-inch 20-gauge 330 Savage, one of his favorites for upland hunting.

The 1100 Remington with adjustable choke handles shots at any range that T.R. Them believes it's sporting to shoot. Here, he waits for some incoming doves.

nating any necessity for unusual finger dexterity, the single trigger makes it simple to come up with a buttstock length that is correct for a single length of pull—something that is, strictly speaking, literally impossible on a two-trigger gun.

The disadvantages of single barrel repeaters are as obvious as the advantages. Their long length, though it appeals to some, bothers others. Not only because it is a nuisance in the thick cover typical of much upland hunting, but also because the forward location of the center of balance makes the gun feel a bit dead and slow to get into action. Most upland hunters try to get around this by selecting the shortest barrel available, usually 26 inches, but even this results in a fairly long gun. The other big problem with single barrels is that they have only a single choke.

Choosing the Right Choke

For beginning hunters we might point out that "choke" is a constriction machined into the muzzle end of the gun's barrel; it works much as a nozzle on a garden hose, to a considerable extent controlling the number of pellets from a shot charge which will strike within a given area at a given distance, usually a 30-inch circle at 40 yards. The cluster of pellet holes is called a "pattern," and is expressed mathematically as a percentage of the shot pellets in the total charge. In shooters' terminology, a barrel which puts 50 percent of its shell's shot charge into the 30-inch circle is bored improved cylinder; 60 percent is a modified choke, and 70 percent or more is full choke. Advanced gunners commonly subdivide these classifications, but since there is often considerable variation between consecutive shots from a given barrel with a given box of shells, and even more variation with different shot sizes and velocities, such refinement seems of dubious value.

The degree of choke is important for it governs the effective range of a shot charge. For fast shooting at short range, a wide open choke—improved cylinder—is best as it delivers a large-diameter pattern which makes hitting easy yet puts comparatively few meat-destroying pellets into the target. The IC boring with a normal load of 7½s or 6s kills well to about 35 yards before patterns become too thin for consistency. Where a lot of opportunities come at beyond that distance, full choke is best as its patterns are large enough for easy hitting at 35 yards or so, yet dense enough to kill well at 55 to 60 yards. The modified choke fits between these two, being neither the best nor the worst at short or long range, in effect a compromise. As such, it has always been a popular boring in single barrel guns, though most upland hunters would be better off with the IC choke. Most upland shots are taken within the IC's effective range, it's easier to hit with than the others, and it doesn't shoot up the game as much.

Adjustable Choke Devices

For many years, every single barrel left the factory with a certain choke built into it and that's how it remained for the duration of its useful life. There were numerous times when a gunner wished he had a more open or tighter barrel than the one he was carrying—birds do flush at different distances—yet common sense told him he had no choice. After all, machined steel is not readily amenable to change. But common sense is no deterrent to wishing, and if enough people want something, someone is going to create it. The result in this case was an adjustable choke that could be attached to the muzzle of a single barrel gun. Actually, several versions appeared, the two best known being the Cutts Compensator and the Poly-Choke. The Cutts uses a series of wrench-installed tubes of different inside dimensions, while the Poly-Choke is a collet type which can be manually tightened or opened. There are other versions of adjustable chokes, and these two have been modified somewhat through the years, but the basic idea remains: to make it reasonably easy for the shooter to change the boring of his single barrel gun in the field or on the claybird range. These units are popular, and they're popular because they work. They can be installed to give the shooter any barrel length he wants, from the legal minimum (by drastically shortening the original before attaching the new unit) to a bit longer than the factory job (the barrel is shortened enough to remove the original choke before installing the adjustable one).

The adjustable choke makes a good slide action or autoloader a true all-around shotgun, one capable of handling woodcock in thick cover without demolishing this tiny bird with a centered pattern, then being quickly adaptable to pass shooting for geese. However, such a gun is not quite perfect. The hunter can choose his choke to match a given piece of cover—IC for ringnecks in a tight corner, say—but once he's done that he has committed himself for the immediate future.

91

Informal claybird shooting can be fun as well as good practice — and the real fun comes after you've given the needle to your buddy for missing an easy shot and he offers you the gun as Jerry Knap is doing to John Madson here. But we know you'll come through John. Winchester's got laws against missing right?

If he glances up to see a rooster that's been kicked out by another gunner blasting downwind some 50 yards away, he's out of luck. He simply doesn't have time to adjust any adjustable choke to take care of such unexpected chances. So what these units do, of course, is let him play the averages. Some shots can't be anticipated, so he just cusses a little when he's caught by them. But overall, the adjustable choke is a very practical answer to most upland shooting chores.

Autos or Pumps?

In a shooting sense, there's little to choose between a slide action and an autoloader. There's a tendency to believe an auto will give faster follow-up shots, and for the average shooter this is probably true. However, an expert with a pump can equal or surpass the rate of fire an autoloader will deliver,

not only getting the shot charges out of the barrel but also hitting with them. Such proficiency, however, takes more than casual practice. Truth of the matter is, though, extremely fast rate of fire is rarely important; what counts most is putting the first pattern on target.

Slide actions, because they are manually operated, will function with any safe, properly loaded shell that fits the chamber—high or low velocity, heavy or light shot charges, whatever. Some autoloaders, though, are more cranky. Because either the recoil generated by the fired shell or the gas from its burning powder is used to work the action, a certain balance of forces is necessary. Enough energy must be transmitted to do the job, but not so much that precisely machined gun parts are subjected to damaging force. Autoloaders are dependent upon near-perfect ammunition if they are to per-

The pattern board not only tells what choke a barrel actually is with a given shell, but also shows whether a shotgun shoots where it is pointed — and whether a double barrel puts both patterns to the same place. Unfortunately, many of them don't.

form perfectly. Any change might have an effect. For instance, at the time of this writing, steel shot is required in certain areas for waterfowl. A friend who uses a top quality 12-gauge auto chambered for 3-inch Magnum shells tells me his gun will not reliably function with factory loaded steel shot ammunition although it works perfectly with lead loads from the same manufacturer. He doesn't know why—and apparently the manufacturer doesn't either, for he's had it back to their shop without positive results—but obviously there's enough difference in the energy effect the steel shot shells have on the gun to alter its functioning. This doubtless will be corrected soon, but it's an example of the kind of problem that can be encountered.

Doubles and Over/Unders

Double barrel guns come in two general designs, side-by-side (S/S) and over-under (O/U). Contrary to popular belief, the O/U was developed first. The S/S is basically a better looking gun as it is shallower in profile. This is most noticeable in the larger gauges, a 12-gauge O/U having a somewhat pregnant look even in models designed to avoid that as much as possible. However, the O/U is more comfortable to carry in one hand precisely for this reason—its narrow width through the action fits the hand better. Its stacked-barrel configuration also appeals to many shooters because it gives the narrow sighting plane they like. One minor drawback is that the depth of the action requires dropping the barrels to a greater distance to reload. Those who prefer the side-by- side often cite its broad muzzle as a plus, claiming it is seen more quickly in thick cover, making for faster alignment, and that its width helps eliminate canting. Both designs come in sidelock or boxlock models, and though guncranks can spend countless evenings arguing the relative virtues of each, so far as most gunners are concerned the whole thing is academic. Both designs have reached a state of near perfection, so there seems little reason for quibbling.

Most current doubles are built with single triggers, a response to popular demand. Most of the time they work, but I've had them double—fire both shots with a single pull—occasionally. A single trigger makes it easy to get a precise stock length, but makes it more difficult to choose the barrel you want to shoot first. A selector, either integrated with the safety or a button near the trigger's top, allows a switch if you have the time and remember to use it. That's usually impracticable. In the end, double triggers seem a more sensible choice.

Double barrel guns have always been popular with some shooters, and in the last decade or so there has been a noticeable swing away from the repeaters to the two-barrel jobs . . . this despite the significantly higher cost of the double. This might suggest that more shooters are economically better off than a generation or so ago, but that isn't the only reason for the switch. Double barrel shotguns have a number of inherent characteristics which make them desirable.

To begin with, there's that second barrel. On those occasions when dependability is important (and in a sense it always is), this design is superior because it's actually two guns in one—two barrels, two locks, two triggers—attached to a single stock. If something happens to one, the other can normally still be used. Such problems don't come up every day, but when they do they can be real, and it's self-evident that a single-shot gun is far superior to a no-shot gun when there's something around that needs shooting.

Having two barrels also means you have two chokes. They're permanent and they're instantly available. Therefore, if they are of the proper boring and you have selected loads to give the optimum performance from each, you can

effectively take game at any reasonable shotgun range, near or far, without disintegrating it at close range or failing to get enough shot pellets into distant targets. Most hunting doubles are bored improved cylinder and modified or modified and full. The former usually comes in 26-inch barrels and is the normal selection for upland hunting, the latter in 28- or 30-inch barrels more suitable for pass shooting on waterfowl. I've no quarrel with the M/F combination for most duck and goose hunting, but would prefer an IC/F choice, still in the short barrel length, for the uplands. By the time you've reached the limit of the improved cylinder's effective range of 35 yards or so, the full choke's pattern is big enough for easy hitting, and of course it reaches out better than the modified boring, so there seems little reason for this compromise choke in a double. Nevertheless, that's the way they're built, so we're stuck with them. A few extremely high-grade doubles are offered in any choke combination wanted, and of course custom-tailored guns are, too. Still, I don't see why the IC/F combination couldn't be phased into regular production in place of the IC/M. It would make the double even more effective in the uplands.

It would be easy to start with an M/F double and have the modified barrel opened up by a good gunsmith, but we'd then end up with 28-inch barrels. Since even 26 inches is longer than necessary, I don't care for that approach. Actually, I'm nitpicking here—an occupational disease of gunwriters. A modified choke with the proper load will handle almost all the longer shots any average gunner should be taking. And if more range is truly necessary for a significant percentage of shots, an afternoon of experimentation with different loads will often turn up one that will deliver full choke patterns from a modified bore.

Two barrels give the opportunity for two different loads, also. It's customary to use lighter shot in the open tube, to get maximum density in the fast-opening pattern, and a heavier size in the tight bore, to maintain energy and penetration out farther. I often use 8s and 7½s (again nitpicking) for woodcock, quail and grouse, 7½s and 6s for pheasants. Early in the season, when shots average closer and birds are smaller, I often use field loads in the open barrel, long-range loads in the tight side, on rare occasions short Magnums. It's possible to make an argument for such choices. But as the season progresses and I get a little tired of such details, I tend to go with 7½s in both sides for the smaller birds, and straight 6s for pheasants. The weight of the charge depends on the gauge, usually an ounce in the 20 unless pheasants are the expected target, when I go to 1⅛ in my standard-chamber M21 Winchester, and 1⅛ or 1¼ in the 16 and 12.

Another advantage of the double is its short overall length for a given barrel length, a result of the lack of an action between barrel and stock. This puts the double's center of gravity between the hands, giving it a livelier, more responsive feel and making it quicker to get on fast flushing game. This is more important than many hunters realize, for most shots in the uplands are the "sudden" kind, best taken by a gunner with good reactions who does his shooting right now. Hesitation often means the intended target is going to vanish behind some sort of cover before the gun is swung into action. This doesn't mean a repeater will never produce kills; most of the time it does. However, after a lot of years of using both basic types, I'm convinced that when fractions of a second mean the difference between a hit and a miss, a well-fitted double has the edge.

The double is faster on the second shot, too, even with a two-trigger gun if it's properly handled. Here, the finger simply slaps the front trigger and slides off it to hit the rear one, the muzzle continuously moving even as the shots are taken. So used, both shots blend into one, just a BOOM-BOOM that

The only way you can be sure what kind of patterns a given gun and load will give is by test firing. Every serious hunter should try this. Results are often surprising.

seems impossibly quick to a person who's never given any thought to the process. I've got a hunch, though I don't know how to prove it, that a two-trigger gun can be fired faster this way than a single-trigger double barrel. With the single trigger, the finger moves rearward, then reverses its direction, then reverses it again. That's essentially the same process as when firing an autoloader or pump, though in those cases the trigger finger's movements are sort of lost in the shuffle of other things. Regardless, on those occasional times when getting a second shot off *fast* is necessary, the double is tops.

A good double (and admittedly not all doubles fall into this category) has something else going for it that, in my opinion, no repeater has—good looks. Opinions about such a thing have to be subjective, of course, but in all honesty I've never seen an autoloader or slide action that excited me esthetically. To me, such guns are shooting machines. Superbly efficient tools. But that says it all. However, the truth of the matter is, most of us spend an awful lot more time looking at our guns than shooting them. And a gracefully designed double has a look about it that no repeater can match, a unity of design and line that's so satisfying the owner can sit and admire it all evening and know he hasn't wasted a minute. I've never been tempted to do that with a repeater, though I grew up shooting both pumps and autos.

Not all doubles have that quality, of course. Some are dogs. But anyone who has the slightest appreciation for a true work of art will realize that's what a good double is, and he'll recognize the quality even if he's not a shooter. There's a forward-leaning, ready-to-go eagerness about it. Even when

it's standing in a rack, it looks like a thoroughbred waiting for the starting bell. This is particularly obvious in a straight-stocked side-by-side with splinter style fore-end or a re-strained beaver-tail. Going overboard here can quickly be too much of a good thing. You just need enough wood to make a comfortable grip for the hand, not enough to use for kindling during a cold snap. Actually, the old splinter fore-end is not a bad design. It looks trim and since the front hand normally cradles the barrels as well as the fore-end, it's perfectly practical except on those rare occasions when a lot of shooting heats up the barrels too much for comfort. (That's the kind of problem we'd all like to have more often!)

Safety First

Somewhere along the line, a choice is made and a hunter buys a gun. He then has to learn to hit with it. If this is just the latest in a long line of firearms, or a new gun to replace an unsatisfactory one, the chore is probably simple, just a matter of adjusting to something a trifle different than what he is used to. Firing a few boxes of shells will make the new gun as familiar as the old one. But for a beginning shooter, a few tips might be helpful.

The first requisite is never-ending awareness that a gun is a non-thinking deadly tool which in a split second can kill you if you handle it carelessly. So make it an absolute habit to immediately open the action of any gun you pick up and check whether it is loaded. Do this every time you pick up a gun, even if you've just laid it down a moment before. Sooner or later that habit will save you embarrassment or trouble—or even your hunting buddy's life. And once you have a gun in your hands, make it another absolute habit never to let it point at anything you don't want to shoot. Countless words have been written about safe gun handling, and they're all worth studying, but the sentence you just read is made up of the most important ones, so read it again. Memorize it. I'm not trying to preach or adopt a holier-than-thou attitude. I've several times found shells in my own supposedly empty guns and I've seen a friend shoot himself during one moment of carelessness, so I know firsthand such things can happen. So take that suggestion seriously. If you follow it under any and all conditions—when you stumble or fall in rough cover as well as when you are kicking through a level weedfield in a line of hunters—you still won't shoot anyone if through some apparently unexplainable circumstance your gun does fire.

Becoming Proficient With the Scattergun

After safety with a firearm comes proficiency. The best way to learn to hit with a shotgun is through personal instruction from a skilled coach. Some European countries have shooting schools where this is possible, but they are scarce enough to be called non-existent in the U.S. Instruction from a friend who is truly a good shot and who knows how and why he hits falls into this category. However, such persons are scarce. Best approach for the average beginner probably is a local claybird range where Skeet and/or trap can be shot. A polite request for a few basic instructions will get things off on the right foot. There are always quiet periods when such requests are no bother, and there are always good shooters who are willing to help out. But as you watch others shoot, don't be influenced by the extreme stances some claybird gunners display. Their radical approaches won't help you a bit in the field—I doubt that they even help on a Skeet range—so ignore them and do your shooting from a comfortable unstrained position.

Some hairy-chested hunters deride claybird shooters, loudly proclaiming that hitting man-made targets is not the same as hitting feathered birds and that they know countless oddballs who never miss at Skeet but can't hit a grouse to save their souls. Somehow, that's not the way I've seen it. I know any number of guys who can outshoot me at Skeet and trap, and the same guys consistently outshoot me on live birds. Why shouldn't they? They fire bushels of shells on the range for every one an average hunter like me fires at game, so they have the kind of gun-handling experience most pheasant shooters never dream of. Furthermore, those "artificial" targets duplicate almost every kind of shot anyone is likely to get in the uplands. Not perfectly, perhaps, for claybirds leave the trap at their top velocity and immediately begin to slow down, which is reverse of a live bird's flight; nevertheless, they are excellent practice, particularly if called for with the gun butt on the hipbone instead of the shoulder and safety "on," so the shooter learns to mount the gun swiftly, smoothly and consistently, simultaneously disengaging the safety, as he would for a flushing bird. He should also use his hunting gun for such practice, not a Skeet or trap gun. The purpose is to gain familiarity and proficiency with the gun which will be used in the field, not just to see how many claybirds can be broken.

It's often possible to get some practice shooting on live birds, too. Barn pigeons and crows are great non-game targets, and since both are nuisances to farmers, careful shooters can often obtain permission to work them over. They're better practice than claybirds for their speeds and directions vary more, they sometimes pass directly overhead, which claybirds don't do, etc. Also, there's a psychological satisfaction in shooting feathered targets that doesn't come from breaking artificial ones.

Carrying Tips

Before you start such shooting, it's a good idea to give some thought to carrying the gun. Unlike Skeet or trap shooting, where you wait with an empty or open shotgun until ready to call for the bird, upland hunting is done with a loaded and cocked gun and you often carry it for hours between shots. So you have to learn some safe, comfortable and convenient ways of doing this. Bird hunters normally walk with the muzzle pointed up and away from themselves and their companions. The gun is quick to get into action from this basic carry as the muzzle has the least distance to move in getting on a flushing bird.

The firing hand is always on the small of the stock, finger slanted across the guard to protect the trigger and the safety on a repeater, thumb holding the safety back if it's located on the tang.

If the gun is carried in one hand, the barrel is usually vertical, butt resting on the hipbone or a row of shells in the vest; or it may simply be carried vertically in the hand for short periods. Often, the gun is rested on the shoulder—trigger up, not the Army right-shoulder-arms carry—barrels slanting back and up so they are pointed higher than the head of anyone in the area if you change direction. From this position, when a bird flushes you snap down on the grip while simultaneously hunching the shoulder a bit to help get the barrel moving, shoving the safety off as the muzzle goes frontward, the fore-end slaps into the left hand, and the butt seats into the hollow of the shoulder. If the butt is resting on the hipbone, you simply shove the muzzle up and away to meet the left hand and settle the butt against the shoulder. It doesn't take long to get off a shot from either version of the one-hand carry.

If expecting a flush, the gun should already be held in both hands, safety on but thumb ready to release it, butt pressed between upper arm and body, muzzle forward and slightly up. From such a position, a perfectly pointed shot can be fired in well under a half-second, so you can often take a bird before it has time to get up much speed. Such shots are often close,

which can be destructive, but if you concentrate on the head-neck area, that's where you're likely to hit, and that's not the eating part anyway.

The gun is often carried in both hands. Again, the muzzle should be upward at a sharp angle for safety. Once in a while, to get the kinks out of the arm muscles, a hunter will carry his gun alongside his thigh, gripped at the balance in the left hand, muzzle forward. The gun can be swept up to firing position reasonably fast, though not as fast as from the other carries described, so this method should not be used when seeing game is likely. This can be a dangerous carry if around others, for as walking direction is shifted to examine different bits of cover, the muzzle will swing in a wide arc and probably point at a companion. For the same reason, unless you are alone, the gun should never be carried across the left arm, at right angles to the direction you're walking. Although a comfortable method, the gun is pointing straight at any friend lined up on your left, and as you walk the muzzle swings forward and backward to endanger anyone in the whole field on that side of you.

It's in the "Swing"

The purpose of carrying a shotgun is to hit something with it. If the target were sitting still, this would be simple. You'd just aim the smoothbore like a rifle and whang off a shot. However, it's long been considered unsporting to shoot sitting game with a shotgun, so the obvious problem for a shooter is to arrange that his moving shot charge will somehow intercept a moving target whose direction of flight can be any one of an infinite number of angles in relation to the gunner, whose distance is unknown, and whose speed—either actual or relative to the shooter—is also unknown.

Three basic methods of doing this have evolved over the years. Not one is perfect. Yet reasonable success can be attained with all, at least under certain conditions. The methods are known as "spot shooting," "sustained lead,"

Greg Grabowicz's modified barrel 870 Remington isn't as good a grouse gun as Chuck Fergus' open-bored 280 Ithaca, but Greg's got the grouse!

and "swing through" or "wipe out."

Spot shooting is defined as firing from a motionless gun at some distance ahead of a moving bird, the plaintive hope being that the paths of the shot charge and the bird will coincide in time and space. This method rarely works, except when the target is moving away at a narrow angle so that the barrel is aligned with the inner edge of the target when the trigger is hit. It should be used only when the bird will vanish in an instant and there simply isn't time for any kind of swing. It's just a flush-boom method. It's the only kind there will be time for on some grouse flushes, and occasional shooters get surprisingly good at it. Making just one shot this way is something most of us will recall with great satisfaction all winter long, even when we know it was largely luck. A wide open choke and a heavy load of fine shot help the odds.

Sustained lead is the method that always seems logical to those with mathematical minds. They immediately recognize that to shoot at a bird by any method you must first see the target and react to it by shouldering the gun. They further recognize that it takes time for the gun's lockwork to function after the trigger is hit, time for the primer to detonate, the powder to be converted into gas and the shot charge to squirt down the barrel and out through space; and that during the total time of these details, the bird will be moving. Secure in the belief that mathematics can solve anything, they conclude that if they just get the muzzle the correct distance ahead of the critter's beak and keep it moving in that relationship while they touch off the trigger, they're bound to get a hit.

The trouble with this system is that it's impossible to know the precise distance, speed or angle of the bird, or the exact time of flight of the shot, so it's actually impossible to know how far ahead you should hold, even if there were some way of recognizing that muzzle/target separation in the first place. Yet hits are made by this method. There are probably a couple of reasons for this success. Though the data fed into the gunner's mental computer is imperfect, he has some help in the shape of the shot charge as it passes through the air. This is not two-dimensional—an impression we tend to have because we've often looked at patterns on a target or illustrations of them in a magazine. Actually, it's a three-dimensional cloud perhaps 3 feet in diameter when viewed end-on, but as much as 8 or 10 feet long. Thus, if the lead is a little bit too great, the bird can still be hit by the tail end of the shot charge after the front pellets miss. Sustained lead shooters also benefit from on-the-spot input. That is, after missing a shot, they change their lead for the next chance at a similar range. If that's a hit, they try it on the following opportunity. This method works best on long passing shots such as doves or ducks tend to give. The most successful sustained lead shooters are those of long experience who have stored up a tremendous amount of data which they seem able to recall at will. I admire people who can shoot this way. I've never in my life hit anything with a sustained lead.

The wipe-out shooters take a different approach. They don't try to figure out anything. They just look at a moving bird, swing along its path from the rear, and when they sense (or subconsciously see) the muzzles passing across the bird, they slap the trigger, never stopping or even slowing their swing. Since it takes time for the lockwork and shell to function (as the sustained lead fellows measure, etc.), by the time everything takes place the wipe-out shooters have a built-in lead that usually is correct because the speed of the swing is influenced by the speed of the target. It's the best method I know for upland shooting. I started this way, instinctively, I guess, with my first shotgun, in the late '30s. Not until years later when I read Robert Churchill's book, *Game Shooting*, did I understand, or even give any thought to, how it works. When I shoot this way, I hit; when I try other methods, I miss.

So I try not to think about anything, but just swing and shoot. That's what works for me. I don't say that it works for ultra-long-range shooting on ducks and geese. I've been told by a fine shotgunner that it doesn't, and I don't have enough experience on these species to argue the point. But in the uplands, it's deadly.

Practice—Practice—Practice

In these days of short seasons, comparatively little game and small bag limits, it doesn't make sense to learn to handle your gun in the field. Opening day offers the most shooting chances, for that's when the most birds are available. To flub these shots is to waste your best opportunities. So you should be completely familiar with your gun before the season opens. This familiarity can be gained by dry firing at home. Everything except the actual shooting can be carried out in a den or bedroom. Even 1 minute of dedicated practice per day will add up to a lot of gun handling over the course of a year, and it will make you a better bird killer without firing a shot.

When no one is around to distract you or make silly comments about being married to Wyatt Earp, get out your shotgun. *Make certain it's empty*. Take a moment to check it for cleanliness and that it's mechanically okay. Give a moment's thought to the skill that went into designing and producing it, and to how fortunate you are to own it. Hell, man, this is *your* gun. In many places around this world, an ordinary guy can't even dream of owning a gun, so take pride in yours. Symbolically at least, it is the most significant possession you have.

Now move into ready position. The muzzle should be slanted forward and up, so that it's hazily within your field of vision when your eyes are focused out beyond where a bird will be rising. Grip the fore-end lightly, with the forefinger of the front hand about parallel to the barrel to aid natural pointing. Snug the buttstock gently between upper arm and body, finger across the guard to protect the trigger. Feet should be spread slightly, for balance and stability against recoil. Pick an imaginary target—the three-way intersection of two walls and the ceiling, perhaps. When a voice within your head says, "Bird," shift your feet to put the target well within the area you can easily cover with the gun, simultaneously pointing the muzzle at the bird with the front hand as the rear one snuggles the buttplate back into the hollow inside the shoulder muscle and your face tilts slightly to press the cheek firmly against the comb. As the gun is moving upward, you thumb off the safety (or press it off with the base of the trigger finger if it's a magazine gun), and even as the butt seats itself you slap the trigger.

You concentrate on the bird, not seeing the gun at all except possibly as a shadowy image in the bottom of your field of view. But because your face is solid against the stock and you and the gun are locked into one unit, your eyes have to be staring down the barrel line, so the shot charge must go where you are looking. Without stopping gun movement in the slightest, you swing to follow a second imaginary bird and hit the trigger again. Sometimes you swing left, sometimes right, or up, down or slanting. Birds fly in all directions and you want to learn to get on each one instantaneously. Don't poke the gun out at different angles from the shoulder to take birds going in various directions; when your cheek leaves the stock, you'll almost always miss. Instead, keep everything locked up as tight as possible and swing the entire body, including the gun, as a unit, preferably rotating on the bootsoles. Practice will bring steady improvement, until the gun seems a living part of you that responds to the stimulus of a target without conscious thought on your part. Eventually it will all boil down to *Flush-Bang-Bang*, the whole thing beginning and ending in a half-second or so. It's all just swing and shoot . . . and dead bird.